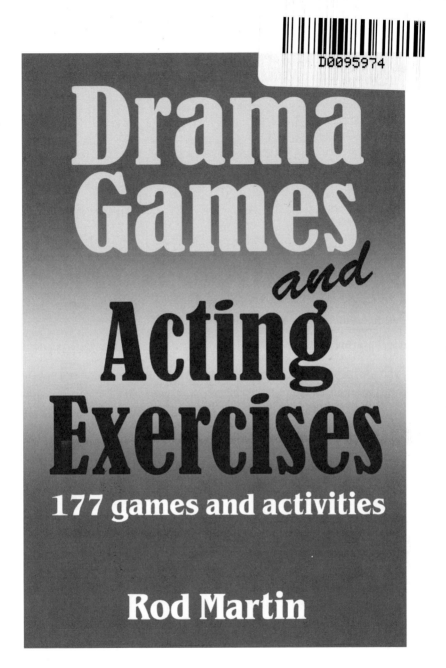

Drama Games *and* Acting Exercises

177 games and activities

Rod Martin

MERIWETHER PUBLISHING LTD.
Colorado Springs, Colorado

Meriwether Publishing Ltd., Publisher
PO Box 7710
Colorado Springs, CO 80933-7710

www.meriwether.com

Editor: Arthur L. Zapel
Assistant editor: Amy Hammelev

© Copyright MMIX Meriwether Publishing Ltd.
Printed in the United States of America
First Edition

Library of Congress Cataloging-in-Publication Data

Martin, Rod.
   Drama games and acting exercises : 177 games and activities for actors /
by Rod Martin.
       p. cm.
   ISBN 978-1-56608-166-5
   1. Improvisation (Acting)--Juvenile literature. 2. Acting--Juvenile
literature. I. Title.
   PN2071.I5M34 2009
   792.02'8--dc22

                                                2009028855

1   2   3   09   10   11

Dedication

I dedicate this book to all teachers willing to include drama in their curriculum. Acting is like practicing life, trying out new ideas and issues in a safe setting. May these warm-ups and exercises help enliven your teaching experience. Teachers are the unsung heroes of our future, giving our children the tools to build an even better world.

Table of Contents

Voice Exercises

Chapter Five:
Public Speaking Made Easy 55

Chapter Six:
Monologues and Duologues 58

Chapter Seven:
Poetry for Performance 63

Chapter One
How Creative Drama Can Enliven the Classroom

Theatre encourages us to share intellectually and emotionally, to explore universal concerns and to renew the spirit. While playing with our fears, hopes, dreams and aspirations, theatre allows us to make meaning that enhances the possibility of our knowing and living successfully with one another.
— The National Theatre Education Project

If each person is helped to enjoy and know what it feels like to use the creative part of themselves when they are young, their eventual appreciation of the arts is richer.
— Brian Way, noted creative dramatist

Creative drama in the classroom is not meant to mimic the competitive nature of the Broadway experience, but should be a supportive environment where the students can practice self expression, touch on issues of relevance to them, and learn about audience manners.

Students of middle school age fear embarrassment and want to be accepted. Drama can help stimulate their learning if it's presented as a *safe zone* where there will be risk, but no ridicule. They can make mistakes and learn from them. They can try out various life scenarios, which can later be discussed with the entire class. For example, they could explore the bullying issue and try different scenes showing how different reactions to conflict can produce different results. In this way, drama can help derail conflict by teaching alternatives within the safety of the classroom. Drama allows the student to be *in the moment,* considering the issues, making choices, even being able to rerun the scene to see other viewpoints and to consider the consequences of various scenarios. In addition, the ability to see things from someone else's viewpoint forms the basis for teaching tolerance and appreciation of cultural diversity.

Theatre teaches us what it's like to "walk in someone else's shoes."
— H.R.H. Fleur

To develop this safe acting environment, the students must understand the boundaries or parameters of each exercise. Some of the important things to mention are safety first, both physical and emotional — no hitting or teasing — only use language that is appropriate for the classroom, and stay away from scenes about sex, violence, or drugs, unless that happens to be the lesson for the day.

Drama can be useful to most disciplines, creating opportunities for hands-on, experiential learning. Creating scenes using headlines from the newspaper for social studies is one example. Performing slow motion replays to teach the rules of a game in PE is another example. Students can even take turns role playing the teacher to see if they can effectively communicate the material the class is covering.

Drama can happen anywhere there are performers and an audience.
Low tech. And high zest.
— George Kon

Remember, just because you as a teacher may not consider yourself much of an actor, don't let that get in the way of having the students try it. They might surprise you. Drama is a powerful tool for a teacher's bag of tricks.

George Kon, noted promoter of drama education said, "Drama is an important tool for any child to learn: to help with their self-esteem, and their language skills. Everybody can be involved from the shyest child to the most outspoken. There's a place for everyone in drama."

Middle school students have lots of energy and are learning to express their individuality. They need to try out new ideas, to explore, and to interact. They move from puppet to playwright, initiating ideas and exploring issues in their own language. They can learn as much from their mistakes as they can from their successes. They are empowered and feel a sense of ownership when it comes to learning. Drama can be the perfect forum for this kind of learning experience.

The word for drama in Greek means "to do." If that doesn't sound like
a recipe for hands-on learning, I don't know what does.
— Rod Martin

Creative drama activities in the classroom will help students develop increased confidence, a willingness to express ideas without shame, the ability to listen to others, to share the spotlight, and cooperate in the act of artistic creation.

Drama is a rehearsal for life.
— Walt Dulaney

In the Fall 1994 volume of *The Kamehameha Journal of Education*, I wrote an article titled, "Improvisation as a Tool for Education." Since most of the exercises in this collection are improvisational, I have included a segment of that article here:

> Participating in improvisations is fun: it has to be for students to be so enthusiastic about it. But what do they learn? They learn they have the power to create. They move from "puppet" to playwright; they no longer mimic the words and ideas of those theater "greats" who came before them, but find a language of their own. They initiate and shape the ideas of their scene. They create the characters, the comedy, the conflict. They are empowered. They take ownership. They are set free to experiment with ideas and language and relationships.
>
> In improvisation, students can test out what works and doesn't work in the realm of human interaction. If a scene doesn't work, they can change it. If a theme is incomplete, they can expand it. When their imagination sparks inspiration and creates magic, they can recapture it, discuss and analyze it, videotape it, write it down, tighten it up, rearrange it until they are satisfied with the final product.
>
> They learn that they each have something to offer. They bring to each scene their own character, ideas, gestures and moods. They learn to cooperate, react and interact. Occasionally, they'll test the limits of what's proper but that can lead to a discussion of values and societal norms. By giving students the freedom to express themselves through improvisation, the teacher can explore with them the dynamics of the interaction and help them gain insights into what they believe and what they care about. Drama can be a rehearsal for life, a way to try out ideas within the safety of "the scene," where students can learn as much from their mistakes as they can from their successes.

The skills improvisation teaches aren't measured by standardized achievement tests. They are demonstrated by increased confidence, a willingness to express ideas without shame, an ability to listen to others, to share the spotlight, and to cooperate in the act of artistic creation. Students who have participated in a variety of improvisations come to know each other better, to see another side of each other. In the process, they become a tighter knit group, more aware of the feelings of others.

Drama is a catalyst for learning, a democratic means
to better understand our world.
— Jamie Simpson Steele

Perhaps most important is that improvisation shifts the focus in the classroom. Students are not asked to memorize or absorb ideas of authors, scholars, scientists, or historians; they become the source of ideas. If, as a teacher, you're looking to make your classroom more student-centered, to give your students a sense of ownership in the learning process, then improvisational theatre exercises will help. You need not give up total control, for you are the one to suggest the improvisations, beginning and ending them. You lead the applause and guide the discussions that follow. Improvisation calls for fast thinking and flexibility, but the rewards can be amazing.

Every child is an artist.
The problem is how to remain an artist after he grows up.
— Picasso

Chapter Two
Warming Up the Actors' Tools

Many people, when they think of drama and acting, think of huge theatres with elaborate lighting, sets, and props. True, these things help embellish any production, but they have little effect on the quality of the acting. Students might be pleased to learn that the real tools of the trade, when it comes to acting, are simply developing the body, voice, and imagination. These three things they have with them always and can work on any time. Just as an athlete prepares for a competition by warming up, so can the actor. Included in this section are many fun activities actors use to tone up and prepare for going on-stage. The warm-ups, particularly the vocal exercises, can help them loosen up and overcome nervousness before giving a speech or class presentation.

Body Exercises

Explain to the students that actors warm up the body for several reasons. It helps them to relax and overcome the pre-performance stage fright or jitters. It helps to prevent injuries because some acting roles require real physical exertion: sword play, acrobatics, dancing, and stunts.

1. Stretching the Face

Ask the students to move everything on their face to the left side, then right, up, and down. This can be fun as a solo performance as well since it usually results in some pretty strange expressions.

2. Neck Rolls

Make sure the students know to take it slow and only stretch as far as feels comfortable.

3. Toe Touches

Have the students bend their knees slightly to prevent pulling tight muscles and stretch slowly, don't bounce. Tell the students to listen to what their muscles are telling them. The muscles will let the students know when they've reached their limits.

4. Side Stretches

Have the students stand in a slightly wider stance than normal and bring one arm up slowly, directly from the side. They then ease into the leaning, trying to feel the stretch from the tips of their fingers, down their arms, sides, and legs. Instruct the students to not twist or turn, but stretch directly to the side. I suggest three stretches to the left, then three to the right, and repeat as long as attention spans hold out. Tell them it's important to do balanced stretching. In other words, equally to both sides or in both directions. Repetition helps, and if they concentrate and relax when stretching, they should be able to go a little farther each time.

5. Balance

This kind of exercise is all about control and being able to control the body, voice, and imagination, which are what acting is all about.

The students stand and the teacher says the following:

How long can you stand on one leg? Try it, then try the other leg. Can you last longer on one particular leg? Besides just lifting a foot, what happens if you hold it out in front of you? Or to the side? What if you rest your raised foot against the other knee? Does it help if you try to breathe slowly? Does it help to focus on a point somewhere in front of you?

6. Pantomime

One way of warming up the actor's body is with pantomime. Pantomime frees the actor from having to come up with lines. No words or attempts at sign language should be part of each student's scene. You can have students pick from a list of possibilities or assign specific scenes that challenge your actors. They can work solo or in pairs — too many cooks may spoil the broth. They can attempt to do the scenes with utmost realism, or try performing with outlandish exaggeration. There is quite a long list of scenarios below, so the teacher can pick and choose what he or she feels is appropriate for the students.

Pantomime Ideas

Be a circus acrobat balancing on a high wire.
You're learning to drive a car for the first time.
Fix a flat tire on a car.
Iron a shirt.
Sew a button.
Pick some wild flowers.

Set a mouse trap and get your finger caught.
You're at a fancy restaurant, but the food tastes awful.
You're chewing bubble gum and you blow a huge bubble
    that pops and the gum sticks to your face and hair.
Collect firewood and start a campfire.
You're driving but getting sleepy behind the wheel.
You're an actor practicing a death scene in many different ways.
Wash the car.
Wash the dog.
You're a heavy metal guitarist in concert.
You're using super glue for a project and get stuck to yourself.
You're a member of the bomb squad defusing a bomb.
You're an astronaut blasting off into space.
Play a musical instrument.
Make a pizza.
Change a baby's diaper.
Put on makeup.
Go fishing.
Lift weights.
Teach your dog tricks.
You're having your ear pierced.
You're a baseball player pitching the ball and then catching the pop-up.
You're shaving and cut yourself.
You're a football player scoring a touchdown.
Learn to surf.
You accidentally brush your teeth with acne cream.
You're eating a specific kind of food and bite your tongue.
Blow up a balloon.
You're skiing down a mountain.
You're a boxer getting beat up pretty badly.
Practice dribbling a basketball.
You're riding on a roller coaster.
You're scuba diving and you see a shark.
Make pancakes from scratch.
You're gambling and losing.
Someone put glue on your seat and you get stuck.
You're a hunter who has second thoughts about shooting an animal.
You're a model in a photo shoot.
You're playing soccer and score a goal.
You're rock climbing but your nose itches.
You're holding your friend's pet snake for the first time.
You're shooting foul shots in basketball. Make some and miss some.

You're eating popcorn at a scary movie.

Make yourself a bowl of ice cream, eat it too fast, and
    get a brain freeze.

Go to the dentist because your tooth hurts.

You're asleep, dreaming of kissing someone, and wake up
    realizing you're kissing your pillow.

You're ice skating and you slip and fall.

You're an old person slowly crossing a busy street.

You're a traffic cop directing traffic.

You're bothered by a mosquito while trying to read a book.

Cook scrambled eggs.

Take pictures with a camera.

Paint a picture.

You're a carpenter pounding a nail and you hit your finger.

You're an astronaut leaving your spaceship to walk on the moon.

You're a worker at a sandwich shop making a sandwich for a
    customer while eating samples without the customer noticing.

You're a shy person at a dance who starts dancing and then gets
    out of control.

You're a surgeon operating on a patient.

You walk your dog and have to clean up after him.

You're washing dishes and accidentally break one.

You're playing a video game and the power goes off.

7. Tug of Reality Rope

Divide the class into partners. Each pair must engage in a tug-of-war contest with an imaginary rope. The goal is to see which pair can most realistically perform the game. Are they observant and lose ground when their partner gains ground? Is there good muscle tension and concentration? Is someone willing to lose?

8. Nonverbal Communication Activity

When it comes to communicating, people tend to believe what they see more than just what they hear, so nonverbal forms of communication are very powerful.

The teacher will suggest several phrases and the students will attempt to communicate those phrases, first with facial expressions, then hand gestures, and, finally, with their body language.

Looks

I'm mad at you.
I'm really mad.
I don't believe you.
I didn't do anything.
You hurt my feelings.

Hand Gestures

You, come over here.
Shhhh.
You stay right there.
I'm watching you.
I can't hear you.
Naughty, naughty.
Stand up, everyone.
Now just hold on.
Use your brain.

Body Language

I'm exhausted.
I'm proud.
I'm conceited.
I'm scared.
I'm bored.
I'm confused.
I'm surprised.
What, you like beef?

9. Melt and Grow, Real Slow

Students first imagine themselves as ice sculptures or statues melting into a pool on the floor. Then they imagine themselves as seeds sprouting out of the earth and growing into huge flowering trees.

10. Choreographers

Besides getting the heart pumping, this warm-up is good for memorization and shows how important repetition is when learning something new.

In a circle, each student makes up a simple dance move. Then the rest of the students copy that move once or twice until they've mastered it. The next student in the circle shows a dance move — twirl, twist, foot stomp, popping — and that is added to the first move. With each addition, the dance becomes longer and more fun.

11. Partner Mirrors

Tell the students they're going to be doing a drama game to test their powers of concentration and observation. Divide the students into partners and have them stand facing each other, far enough apart that if they both put their arms out forward they won't be touching. Tell them they have to maintain eye contact the entire time and cannot turn away from each other. One of the partners is picked to be the leader of the mirroring. Tell that leader to move as if in slow motion so his partner can follow without becoming confused. After a minute or two, have the other partner be the leader. For an advanced exercise, each of the partners can try leading at the same time.

12. Real and Big

This is a pantomime exercise where the students first mime an activity, such as brushing one's teeth, as realistically as possible. Then, they demonstrate the same activity but do it really big, exaggerated, and huge.

13. Superstar

Play some contemporary music and have the students lip sync and play air guitar to it. For an advanced exercise, switch between all kinds of music and the students can mime playing an instrument or being back-up dancers in a music video.

14. Focus Frisbee

The teacher mimes holding a Frisbee that will be thrown around the circle. Explain the importance of first making clear eye contact with the person to whom the student intends to toss the Frisbee. If the students are just getting to know each other, the teacher can suggest they say their own name when catching the Frisbee. Once a student has had a chance to catch and throw the Frisbee, he should put his hands behind his back so that everyone gets a chance to participate and no one is left out.

Once the students have mastered the game, they can try the same thing, without names, without miming throwing the Frisbee, using only eye contact to pass the *focus*. When playing this game, it's a good time for the teacher to mention the importance of focusing on the person who is giving directions or performing during the drama exercises. When not actively saying or doing something during an exercise, the other students become the audience. There should be no distracting side talking.

15. Walks That Talk

Clear a path around the room for all the students to walk in the same direction. As the students walk, the teacher will be giving them suggestions that will affect their body language and the way they walk.

Walks

Walk like you're looking for something.
Show that you're walking in the rain.
Walk like you're a dancer.
Walk like you're exhausted.
Walk on tiptoe, very quietly.
Walk like you're in a hurry.
Walk like you're mad about something.
Walk like you're in pain somewhere.
Walk stiff legged.
Walk like a giant.
Walk like you're afraid of something.
Walk like you think you're so great.
Walk in slow motion.
Walk like you're really happy.
Walk like you're walking into a strong wind.
Walk like you are a robot.
Walk like a bow-legged cowboy.
Walk with tiny steps.
Walk with huge strides.
Walk like you're in a marching band, playing an instrument
    of some kind.
Walk like you're depressed about something.
Walk like you're walking across hot sand.

16. Small Change

This warm-up is done with partners and focuses on one's powers of observation.

The partners stand facing each other. One is chosen to be the Observer, and the other the Changer. After less than a minute of observing, the Observer must turn away while the Changer makes a very small change in his appearance — moves a shoelace, removes an earring, changes his hair slightly. The Changer then tells the Observer he can turn around and try to figure out what has changed. Sometimes he gets it and sometimes he doesn't. It's a challenge.

17. Find the Leader

This warm-up involves the whole class. Tell them they are going to participate in a game of follow the leader with simple, repetitive gestures and sounds. One person is chosen as the Guesser and must leave the room or enter *the cone of silence*: eyes closed, hands over the ears, humming loudly. While the Guesser is out of the room or in the cone of silence, a Leader is chosen and the class stands in a circle. The Leader starts the movement and/or sound before the Guesser returns. The Leader must change the movement or sound several times during the course of the game and not get caught. The Guesser stands in the center of the circle and has only three guesses to find the Leader, or a new Guesser and Leader will be chosen. Be sure to instruct the class not to always look at the Leader, or the Guesser can just follow their eye contact and find the Leader too easily. The leader should not change the moves when the Guesser is looking at him.

18. Alpha-aerobics

Have the students use their whole bodies to spell out the letters of the alphabet. They can work solo or with partners. The teacher calls out the letters to keep things moving. The teacher can also call out the letters more quickly for advanced play.

19. Balancing Act

Have the students partner up and experiment with the many and various ways one can *support* a partner through leaning, stretching, and balancing. Choose several pairs to demonstrate their technique for the whole group.

20. Quiet Time?

Ask the students to stand or sit perfectly still and concentrate only on what sounds they can hear. Are they, themselves, able to be quiet? Can they hear noises in the room or sounds from outside? Can they hear people breathing? Does it help if they close their eyes?

21. Tense and Relax

The teacher has the students sit or stand comfortably, each in their own space. The teacher then suggests various muscles to tense and then relax. Deep, slow breathing should accompany this exercise. Work from the face down to the feet.

22. Photo Touch Up

Six students are chosen to form an unusual *frozen tableau,* or freeze frame picture. The rest of the class is told to observe every detail of the picture. Then they're told to close their eyes while the teacher or a student volunteer makes three small changes in the picture by slightly repositioning the members of the tableau. When told to open their eyes, the students doing the observation must raise their hands if they'd like to guess one way the picture has be touched up. After three correct guesses, a new group can be chosen for the tableau and the guessing continues.

23. Where's My Jump Rope?

This one will get the students' hearts pumping.

Have them perform solo jump rope. Then have the jumper work out between two rope spinners who encourage the jumper to keep going and even try some tricks. The ropes are imaginary, but the jumping will feel real enough.

Try other well-known games with imaginary objects. Try dodge ball, soccer, catch, or flag football. Some games may have to be played outside.

24. Slow Motion Tag

Tell the students the goal of this exercise is to move in slow motion and to make sure that everyone gets a chance at being *it.* A person can only be *it* once per game. The teacher picks someone to be *it* to start the game. The students will be tempted to hurry to get away. Remind them that they have to move slowly and that it's OK to be tagged *it.* Once a person has had a turn at being *it,* they can retire to the sidelines but it's more fun if they stay in the game to get in the way. The students have to pay attention to make sure they don't tag a person more than once.

A variation of the game would be to have only one person be *it* and have the people tagged freeze in position until everyone has been frozen.

25. Find, Feel, and Move

Where the awareness goes, the energy flows.

Students may do this awareness exercise sitting at their desks or standing in a circle. The teacher reads aloud the following things they should focus their attention on:

Notice the temperature in this room. Do you feel warm? Cool? Is it humid? Is there a breeze?

Now concentrate on your feet. Feel them before you move them. Try to move only your toes. Now be aware of your hands. Move just one finger. Now move two fingers that are not next to each other. Make a fist, then stretch the fingers wide apart. Now move your hands at the wrist. How many different directions will your hands move?

Now be aware of the hair on your head. Can you make your scalp move without touching it? Can you move your ears? Now move your eyes in all directions, even cross-eyed. How many ways can you move your nose? How many shapes can you make with your mouth?

Now experiment with moving your neck and shoulders.

For a challenge, try to move all those different parts of the body at the same time. How many can you move? Start with slow motion and then speed things up.

26. Last Comic Walking

This physical warm-up and improv is based on Monty Python's sketch, "The Bureau of Funny Walks."

Tell the students this scene is an audition for a new talent show called, "The Last Comic Walking." Three students are chosen to be judges with the following characteristics: one loves every audition and always finds something complimentary to say; one is rude, negative, and hard to please; and one speaks pidgin, ebonics, or with a southern drawl and always wanders off the topic of judging.

Students then volunteer or are chosen to be the contestants auditioning for the show. Tell them not to repeat any type of walk that has been previously demonstrated by another student. The winner may be chosen by *the studio audience* — class members — with a vote, or the teacher, consulting with the judges, may announce the winner.

27. The Wave

Have the students form lines or a circle. Tell them to begin in a crouching position, then they rise sequentially, like the opposite of falling dominoes. They rise to fully standing with arms and fingers stretched to the sky as the wave moves down the line or around the circle.

28. What's Going On?

This group warm-up can involve everyone and might look like a modern dance recital.

Ask the students to move, stretch, exercise, and/or dance doing a variety of movements — nothing suggestive — that continually change their positions. When the teacher calls "freeze," everyone holds the position they are in. The teacher then asks a few of the students to explain "What's going on?" and they must justify their position. This is a good imagination stretcher. The exercise then continues until several, or all of the students, have had a shot at an explanation.

29. Join on In (Partners)

This is a warm-up for partners to perform one at a time in front of the class. One student in the pair is quietly given a suggestion for a mimed activity or they make up their own and they begin acting it out. As soon as the partner figures out what's going on, they must find a way to add to the mime. Repeat until all pairs have performed in front of the class.

30. Prop Me Up

The teacher and students bring in a variety of unusual props for this exercise. Each prop is presented and volunteers are asked to use that prop, to show, not tell. For example, a broom can become a golf club, clarinet, javelin, etc. If some students are shy or can't think of anything, the teacher can ask them to act out a suggestion from the other students.

An advanced form of the game is to use the props in some way in a two or three person scene.

Examples of props:

A towel

String or rope

A cardboard box

A Frisbee

A pillow

31. Now Hear This

Two groups of students compete, with eyes closed, to correctly identify sounds the teacher and students make. This improv features attentive listening and awareness.

Sounds
Pencil tapping
Ripping paper
Finger snaps
Fan
Typing
Moving a desk

32. Pass It On

Have the class form a circle. Tell the students to use their best miming to pass selected imaginary objects. At the start, the teacher can say the name of the object out loud for all to hear.

For a more advanced exercise, show, but don't tell, the students what the object is until it's gone all around the circle.

Imaginary Objects
Ice cube
Kitten
Cockroach
Rope
Rubber band
Snake
Bomb
Spaghetti
Tub of water
Weights
Helium balloon

33. Food Fun

This warm-up makes us look at the things we do every day, perhaps in a different way. Having to exaggerate goes beyond personal observation and to the imagination.

Students work solo or in small groups. First, they demonstrate eating a specific food, silently. Then they eat the same food with as much detail as possible, adding sound.

An advanced version is for the students to eat that specific food in an exaggerated or big way.

34. Sound and Movement Metamorphosis

This warm-up covers both body and voice.

Have the class stand in a circle. A student or the teacher starts this warm-up by standing in the center of the circle and making both a sound and a movement that is repeated. The students in the circle start doing that same sound and movement, remaining in the circle. Then the leader goes and stands in front of someone, choosing him to take his place as leader in the center of the circle. The sound and movements should not stop. When the newly chosen leader gets to the center of the circle, he must transform the original sound and movement into something new by changing each slightly; that's where the metamorphosis comes in. The warm-up can continue until everyone has a chance to lead, or they get worn out.

Voice Exercises

35. Humming

I like to start vocal warm-ups with some simple humming.

Ask the students to take a deep breath and then hum on the lowest note they can make and repeat. Next, ask them if they can *move the sound around* in their head while humming, bringing it up into the nose, or deep in the throat.

Let them find out what happens if they try to hold their nose and hum — hopefully they'll stop humming before they blow their eardrums.

36. Sighs

Tell the students to take a really deep breath and then let it out in a big, loud, long sigh going from high in pitch to low. Demonstrate for them and then have them try several times. Then do some from low to high. This helps relax the vocal cords and the sighing can also help ease the feelings of stage fright.

37. Lions

Have the students make big roaring sounds while slowly rolling their heads, first to the left, then the right. Sounds silly, but I learned it in my college acting class.

38. Stretching the Mouth

Tell the students to say the vowels a, e, i, o, u opening their mouths as wide as they can when they say them. The students should be able to feel the muscles around their mouths stretching as they do this. Repeat this at least three times then take it up a notch by adding a variety of prefixes to those vowels. For example, add "str" as a prefix: stra, stre, stri, stro, stru. Or the prefix "gl": gla, gle, gli, glo, glu. Other examples: fra, fre, fri, fro, fru, na, ne, ni, no, nu, pa, pe, pi, po, pu, za, ze, zi, zo, zu.

39. Articulation and Enunciation

It's the actors' job to perform the script writer's words as clearly as possible so they can be understood. Tongue twisters are a fun way to practice pronunciation. The teacher can make up tongue twisters relating to the students names, or things covered in class content. It's a good idea to let the students try to come up with some, but it's best to have them write their ideas down first and hand them in, then the teacher picks the best and avoids any that might be offensive.

A list of tongue twisters I've enjoyed over the years:
Peter Piper picked pilau papaya.
Red rubber baby buggy bumpers.
I spilt lemon liniment on the aluminum linoleum.
The Sheik's sixth sheep's sick.
Round and round the rugged rock, the ragged rascal ran.
    (Now try it rolling each "r.")
I've got a Swiss wristwatch.
She sells short spotted sox.
Charming Charlie chewed cheekfuls of chewing gum.
My mother met Monique in a unique New York boutique.
Red leather, yellow leather. (Keep repeating.)
Toy boat. (Keep repeating.)
A crop of poppies in a copper coffee pot.
I'm confident a curtained cubicle can counteract your
    incredible constipation.
I wonder which way is the westerly windward wind.
There's more in the middle of an egg McMuffin than the egg
    in the middle of the muffin.
Nancy knew nine Norwegian knuckleheads.
Terrible teenage twins are two times too tall to tell tall tales.
Better beware of big black biting Bulgarian bedbugs.
Charlie chose crispy chicken over original recipe.

Don't dilly dally when digging Daphnee's dirty ditch.
Fred's friend Fiona fought five fresh flounder while fishing.
Please pass the tie wire pliers.
Moses supposes his toeses are roses.
Cute cuddly kittens. (Repeat numerous times.)
Little Lucy licks a lemon lollipop.
I told the waiter to page Pualani later.
Six shining coins. (Repeat several times, fast.)
Pre-shrunk shirt sizes. (Repeat.)
Three tall trees. (Repeat.)

40. Pass the Whisper

This is essentially the old game *Telephone.*

To begin, tell the students the focus of this exercise is to show the importance of speaking clearly to avoid misinterpretation or misunderstanding of the message.

The students form a circle or line across the front of the room and the teacher begins a whispered message. The students pass the message down the line.

For advanced play, tell the students they cannot repeat the message. The messages may also get longer and more complex as the game and the students' skills progress.

41. Sentence in a Circle

Have the students form small circles of four to seven people. Each circle is given a list of sentences. After one student reads the first sentence aloud three times, the others in the circle say that phrase with each student contributing only *one syllable* at a time around the circle.

The phrases can be review questions for a test, guidance issues, or any points the teacher wants to emphasize.

Examples:
Do unto others as you would have others do unto you.
Bullying is unacceptable behavior.
Dental hygiene is everyone's responsibility.
A fool and his money are soon parted.

42. Back at You — Phrase Reaction

For this vocal warm-up, students may work with partners or in a circle. The first student makes a statement and his partner, or the next in line in the circle, makes a statement that is a direct reaction to what the first person said. The focus of the exercise is to react quickly and honestly, which is a skill that will come in handy for improvs.

Warn the students not to say hurtful things, but also remind them that all statements should not be taken literally and some may seem outrageous just to provoke a strong reaction. If the teacher feels something inappropriate has been said, he should call a halt right then and there to discuss it and provide a more appropriate suggestion.

43. Thanks for the Memories

The students sit or stand in a circle. The teacher announces a topic — it could be a lead-in for the day's lesson — such as colors, flowers, cities, countries, musical groups, etc. Around the circle, each person thinks of one thing or personal experience associated with that topic. The next person must summarize what the first person said and then add his own comment. The list grows longer with each person. This can show how repetition aids memorization.

44. Act Out a Word

To prepare for this activity, which is great for vocabulary development, have the students help list words that would be fun to act out. Once an appropriate list has been completed, a student is chosen to act out one of the words.

First, he should try to mime the word, making no sound. Then he tries again, this time adding sound, but not saying the word. Finally, he acts out the word and can say the word in any way and as often as he likes.

Discussion may follow each performance with students offering suggestions of other ways the word could be presented.

Words

Explosion	Fountain	Lava
Sunrise	Surprise	Hurricane
Heartbreak	Confusion	Forgetful
Insect	Hunter	Wounded
Lost	Terrified	Indecision
Hidden	Kung Fu	Gesture
Flirting	Macho	Squirm

| Giggle | Freedom | Staring |
| Robbery | Pour | Float |

45. Double Talk

Pick a topic from current events, something happening at the school, or something of interest to the students. Divide the class into partners. This warm-up starts as a conversation between each set of partners until the teacher calls out "double talk," and then both partners speak at the same time, trying not to be distracted by what the other is saying.

For an advanced game, the partners should try to borrow words from the other partner's story and incorporate them into their own, hopefully using it in a different context.

46. Emotional Outburst

The students stand in a circle. The teacher calls out an emotion and each person around the circle, like dominoes, makes a sound or statement expressing that feeling.

Emotions
Love
Fear
Disgust
Jealousy
Joy
Hate
Surprise
Hurt
Sorrow

47. Pass the Phrase around the Circle

Standing in a circle, ask the students to pass a phrase to the person next to them. They must keep the same exact wording, but encourage them to experiment with the tone, rate, and inflection of how they say the phrase. Demonstrate for them how the same phrase can have different meanings depending on how it is said. For example, "So nice to see you" can sound friendly or sincere, but if said with hesitation can show that one is not so pleased. It's very important from the start to remind the students to stay focused and that means paying attention only to the person who is speaking the phrase. There should be no side discussion or practicing. Each person deserves to have everyone's attention while performing.

21

Phrases

You look marvelous.
What, you like beef?
You hurt my feelings.
You're in trouble now.
You did what?
This is for you. (Tell the students to clearly show through
    their gestures just exactly what the *this* is.)
I really want to thank you for what you did.
I feel sick.
Are you talking to me?
Wurd up, my homey.
Who do you think you are?
I can tell what you're thinking.
What are you going to do now?
Are you listening to me?
I don't believe a word you say.
Are we having fun yet?
I've got a pain right here. (Each spot should be different. No going
    for inappropriate areas.)
What are you looking at?
Can you do this? (This one is fun for weird faces and sounds.)
I'm in love.
You make me so mad.
I am so sorry.
Are you alright?
I feel good.
That's a bummer, dude.
That is like, so weird.

48. Same Line, Many Ways

Around the circle, everyone must say the same line, but the teacher offers suggestions on how to say it. The lines can be suggested by the teacher or the students can make up their own.

Suggestions on how to say the lines:

Suspensefully	Loudly
Lazily	Angrily
Softly	Sadly
Bored	Suspiciously
Silly	Nervously

22

Excitedly	Like a news anchor
Like a commercial	Like it was a line from a rock song
Like a snob	Like a little kid

49. Listen to Your Director

This exercise helps students with their listening skills.

The teacher can make the point that an actor must listen and follow the directions of the Director if he wants to keep his part. Place objects and obstacles in the front of the room — i.e., chairs, erasers, fans, books, boxes, etc. One student is chosen as the Director, one is chosen as the Actor, and one as the Stage Manager. The Director stands at one end of the obstacle course and the Actor at the other end. The Director tells the actor to close his, or he is blindfolded. The Stage Manager then rearranges the objects. Next, using only verbal instructions, the Director guides the Actor in slowly crossing the obstacle course.

For advanced play, the director gives the directions only once before the actor begins crossing the obstacle course.

50. Conversations That Make Sense(s)

This vocal warm-up and improv is done with partners. The partners are given a topic to discuss and are told to follow the teacher's side coaching. The teacher begins by saying, "Focus on the *sights* involved in the topic." The students then attempt to describe as many visual images related to the topic as possible. Next, the teacher calls out, "Now focus on the *sounds.*" The topic should remain the same, but the students now focus on including sounds related to the theme of the conversation. Do the same for the senses of touch, smell, and taste.

This exercise can help students with their writing skills, teaching them the importance of including sense imagery detail for greater clarity.

51. Unexpected Turns

Three students are chosen to tell a story that keeps making unusual turns each time the teacher calls for a change of storyteller. Warn them not to kill off their characters because they need to keep the story going. Tell them not to rush, the fun is in the details. Take the time to explore the new direction the story is headed. Add new characters. Change the location. Come up with new conflicts.

52. Singing

If the teacher can sing or isn't embarrassed to try, he leads the students through some simple scales and octave jumps to see if they can match the notes.

Some songs that are fun to sing:
John Jacob Jingleheimer Schmidt
Row, Row, Row Your Boat (As a round)
She'll Be Coming 'Round the Mountain
Bingo
Itsy, Bitsy Spider
This Land Is Your Land

53. Levels of Laughter

Have the students place their hands on their diaphragms, just below the rib cage, to feel the muscle that helps force air out of the lungs. Have them repeat the following, forcing the sound out, "ha, ha, ha," "ho, ho, ho," and "hey, hey, hey!" It takes good breath control to project to the back of a big auditorium or classroom.

Chapter Three
Getting to Know Each Other

54. Stage Names

In a circle, everyone introduces themselves saying, "My real name is _____, but my stage name is _____." It's fun and simple. The students can make up imaginary names, like Pop McSicle, or use the names of famous people.

55. Greetings

Students form two lines facing each other. The teacher should fill in if there are an odd number of students. Tell the students to greet the person they're facing. First, they do it naturally, as themselves, being sure to exchange first names. Then the teacher gives them suggestions on different ways to greet each other.

Greeting

Like long lost friends
Like snobs
Like old enemies
In a rush
Like old people
Like little kids
Being overly polite or complimentary
Being extremely shy
At a really loud concert
Like spies
Like robots
Like a movie star and a fan
Like an adult to a baby
With a case of "the giggles"

56. Find Someone Who ...

The students go around the room, shake hands with everyone, and introduce themselves. The students can then ask who they just met questions to fill in their lists. The person who meets enough classmates to fit the most categories wins. Write the first name of each person who fits a statement on the line at the start of each sentence. Only one category should be filled in with each encounter. Students may go back to re-interview someone only after they have met all the other students.

Sample statements:

_____ knows a few Hawaiian words.

_____ has an unusual pet.

_____ is left-handed.

_____ is an only child.

_____ has a stepsister or stepbrother.

_____ is new to this school.

_____ has been camping.

_____ has caught a fish.

_____ is the oldest child in his or her family.

_____ has a collection of some kind.

_____ has been on a sports team.

_____ has broken a bone.

_____ has a birthday the same month as you.

_____ lives in an apartment.

_____ wears glasses or contacts.

_____ plays a musical instrument.

_____ can whistle.

_____ is a good singer.

_____ enjoys reading.

_____ is a good video game player.

_____ has his or her own computer.

_____ has eaten an unusual food.

_____ knows how to cook.

_____ does his or her own laundry.

_____ has had a paying job.

_____ hasn't met you before.

_____ is wearing some new clothes or shoes.

_____ has lived in more than one place.

_____ has been to another country.

_____ has different colored eyes than you.

_____ can surf.

_____ owns a boogie board.

_____ has been to a music concert.

_____ has his or her own cell phone.

57. The Name Game

If the students are just beginning to learn each other's names, this game can help.

Students think of an adjective that starts with the same letter as their name, like Rowdy Rod or Jumpin' Justin. Or, they can say their name and tell one of their favorite things to do, "I'm Emily, and I love going to Disneyland." Making associations helps to remember their names. Every so often, the teacher can ask one of the students in the circle to tell the names of the four closest students. When everyone's had a chance, the teacher can ask if someone can say everyone's name.

58. Two Truths and a Lie

Divide the class into two teams. One member of a team starts the game by making three statements about himself: two that are true and one that is a lie. The other team tries to guess which statement is a lie. Then it's the opponent's turn to have one of their players make three statements. A team scores a point for each correct guess and the team with the most points after everyone has had a turn to make three statements wins. Warn the students not to make the lie so outrageous that it is easily guessed. Prizes are not necessary for the winners. The fun of playing the game should be a reward in itself.

59. Follow the Leader's Mood

For this exercise, the students are told to mingle as a group, interacting with as many students as possible in the class. One person is chosen as the leader. That person demonstrates a particular mood in every encounter he has with the other students during the mingling. The others must figure out what that mood is and then do likewise as they talk to the other students. They should not say the same things, but try to find their own way of expressing that particular mood.

Throughout the exercise, the teacher may call out a student's name to choose a new leader. If the students need help in picking a mood, a list can be posted on the board and discussed before the game begins.

Moods

Angry	Frustrated	Shy
Excited	Worried	Lovestruck
Exhausted	Suspicious	Envious
Defeated	Shocked	Bored
Disgusted	Hurried	Terrified
Talkative	Bullied	Egotistical
Crazy	Sad	Snobby

Chapter Four
Improvisation

Asking oneself "what is my motivation" is the basis for scene study and an important question to consider when making decisions.
— Mary Kabel-Gwin

Guidelines for Making Improvisation Work

The teacher should give the students the following guidelines when doing improv:

- Accept what you're given, don't deny it. If a person in your scene says that you're his best friend, work with that. Agree and add to that.
- Never deny information given. Your fellow actor is trying to lead the scene somewhere, and if you deny what's going on, you'll never get there.
- Be changed by new information. If your fellow actor mentions your broken leg, act like you do and continue to do so. No miraculous healings.
- Take turns. Give all the actors in the scene with you a chance to say something, to add to the scene, and to take it somewhere. If they're really quiet, ask them a question to help include them.
- Stop while you're ahead. If the scene has lasted a few good moments, don't push it. End on a good line or a laugh. Don't extend the scene until it dies a slow death. And if it's just not working at all, stop at the first opportunity. You can always say, "Time for our big death scene," and everyone dies in a different way.
- Follow the action. If your fellow actor is trying to take the scene in a particular direction, go along and see what happens. Don't try to steer it your own way. You're not the only one with ideas, you know.
- Offer a direction. If a situation or relationship has been established for a scene but it doesn't seem to be going anywhere, make a suggestion or add some new information. This can be a question, a complication or problem, or a discovery.
- Have some interesting questions, conflicts, or discoveries planned out ahead of time and use them when needed. You don't always have to work off the top of your head, extemporaneously.

Assessing Drama Performance

Improv and acting in general aren't easy to evaluate. Teachers come to know their student's strengths over time and should consider their ability, growth, and effort when judging their performance. At the end of this chapter on page 54 is a sample grade sheet. It is just a suggestion for things to consider when assessing drama performances. The teacher can pick and choose from the sample or create his own.

Improv Scene Suggestions

The following list of scene suggestions will help with the improv games in this chapter if you or the class can't come up with an idea.

Clothes shopping
Learning to swim
Learning to drive a car
Surfing lessons
Painting a house
Building a fire
Fishing
Riding on a roller coaster
Changing a flat tire
Operating a popcorn maker that gets out of control
Parachuting for the first time
Going to the doctor for a pain that keeps moving around in the body
At a photo shoot with models
Morning rituals in getting ready for school
At the hairdresser or barber shop
A movie star being made up as an alien or monster
Having a tooth removed by the dentist
Doctor Frankenstein bringing his monster to life
A baby-sitter with bratty kids
Ending a relationship while on a roller coaster
Riding on the bus over a very bumpy road
Suffering from a heat wave
On a stagecoach in the Wild West, attacked by robbers or Indians
Riding in a limo for the first time
A backseat driver in a car or on a motorcycle
Abducted by aliens into their spaceship
Having trouble with a vending machine
Invited to dinner but the food tastes awful
Trying to borrow money from a friend with no good reason for
    needing it

Someone in the scene is just too nosy about other people's business

The lights go out in the house at night

Finding a melted candy bar in your pocket

Mountain climbing and someone forgot his food and water

Changing a baby's diaper

Explaining to the teacher why your homework is late

A teen trying to convince his or her parents to accept his or her "unusual" boy or girlfriend

Teen telling his or her parents about a dented fender

Bargaining with your parents for a higher allowance

Discussing curfew options with a parent

Discussing getting a tattoo with parents

Fighting over the TV remote control

Parents discussing what to say to their child about teen drinking

Bringing home a bad report card

Out on a date, the guy forgets his wallet

Two people meet and think they know each other but find out they're mistaken

Stopped by the police because you fit the description of a shoplifter

A waiter spills the soup on a customer

Trying to impress your date's parents with evermore outrageous lies

Calling someone for a date and realizing you've got a wrong number

A news anchor reporting on an explosion at a science lab

Robots complaining about their owners

A talk show host interviewing aliens who have landed on Earth for a peace mission

You get a notice to report to the principal's office, start making excuses for the mistakes you've made, then find out you're there to receive an award for most improved student

Taking Tarzan, fresh from the jungle, to the mall for his first time

Teens being followed around by an annoying little brother or sister

Getting caught trying to sneak out of the house

Two people in jail trying to impress each other with how tough and streetwise they are

New student bragging about how great his or her last school was

Teens telling the new student what they have to do to fit in with their clique

Two people find out they're going to a dance with the same date

Exploring a haunted house

On African safari, you run out of gas in the middle of the jungle

An old person who is hard of hearing keeps misunderstanding what people say

Giving advice to your peers in a graduation speech
In the audience at a wrestling match
Animals that can talk
Giving directions in a mall
At a Nascar race
Bad acting in a soap opera
A coach trying to cheer up a team that is losing badly
You're a student teacher on your first day teaching
A police officer trying to get a description of a robber from a
    witness who doesn't speak English
You're an artist who sees "art" in everyone and everything around
    you
Cheering up a friend who's depressed
Trapped on a deserted island
A visit to the psychiatrist
Malfunction in the spacecraft
Beans for dinner on a submarine

60. Hitchhiker

This is a fun improv and an easy one for beginners.

All that's needed are three chairs to suggest a car. Everything else is done with pantomime. One actor sits in the front left seat and assumes the role of the driver, remembering to keep his hands on the wheel and look at the road now and then. The driver sees a hitchhiker standing with his thumb out on the side of the road and offers him a ride. That actor mimes opening the car door — you can't walk through steel — and sits in the front right passenger seat. The main idea behind this improv is that everyone in the car becomes like the hitchhiker. If the hitchhiker has a cold, everyone in the car has a cold. If that hitchhiker just robbed a bank, they all become bank robbers.

Next, another hitchhiker enters and sits in the single chair behind and between the front two. Three people at a time trying to talk in this scene are more than enough. The driver then must come up with a reason to leave the car, hopefully having something to do with what's going on in the scene at the moment. For example, if the last hitchhiker picked up was a fashion model, the driver might leave saying he needs to buy some makeup or go to a sale at the mall.

This improv gives students a chance to experiment with building a character and trying out new voices and mannerisms. Remind them to take turns talking. If they all speak at once, no one can be heard clearly.

Types of Hitchhikers
A bank robber
A valley girl
A rich snob
A blind person
A person with poison ivy
A person with an imaginary friend

61. Tag Team Freeze

This improv can be fun, funny, and surprising. It consists of fast changing scenes and gives everyone a chance to get in on the action.

Here's how it works: Two actors are told to show a sport suggested by the audience or teacher. After a short time, the teacher calls, "freeze" and the actors freeze in position. It works best when the actors try to make big, broad movements and get themselves into interesting positions and levels. Once frozen, another actor is chosen or volunteers to *tag out* one of the frozen actors and assume the position they were in, but then starts a totally different and unexpected situation. That scene continues until the teacher again calls, "freeze" and the process of changing actors continues.

Here's an example: Let's say the two actors started with a tennis game, and get to arguing about who has the best racquet. They end up pantomiming that they both are holding the same racquet up high and "freeze" is called. The new actor tags one of them out, grabs hold, and says, "Don't let go of the rope! We can make it to the top of this mountain if we just hold on." The actor who was left from the tennis scene then switches characters and goes along with the new idea that has been offered.

This improv helps with their miming skills since no props are used, only imagined. It takes cooperation and fast thinking. If the other actors waiting to join in the scene don't have an idea of how to change the scene, it's OK for the teacher to offer a suggestion. Hopefully, in time, even the shy ones will be able to come up with their own ideas.

62. Two Tongues Tied

In this improv, the actors can say only two words at a time. After the first actor speaks, he must wait until the second actor says his two words before the first actor can say his next two. Tell the students the object is to try to make it sound normal — not Tonto speaking, "Me go," or "Me hungry." They also shouldn't try to take a long sentence and try to say it in two words. This is usually just a two-person improv. If more people are included it gets hard to keep track of whether each person has said his two words.

Example:
STUDENT 1: How're things?
STUDENT 2: Not bad.
STUDENT 1: That's good.
STUDENT 2: What's up?
STUDENT 1: I'm worried.
STUDENT 2: What about?
STUDENT 1: My grades.
STUDENT 2: No kidding?
STUDENT 1: I'm flunking.
STUDENT 2: What subject?
STUDENT 1: Math. Science.
STUDENT 2: That's trouble.
STUDENT 1: You bet.
STUDENT 2: You study?
STUDENT 1: Not much.
STUDENT 2: It figures.

Situations

The submarine you're on has sprung a leak.
The people who designed your spaceship forgot to include a bathroom.
You run out of gas on the way to a big concert.
Someone has managed to Super Glue his hand to his head.
The soda machine has kept your money.
Someone has lost his pet iguana.
You're a kid at the principal's office for too many tardies.
The teacher catches a kid cheating on a test.

63. Questions Only

The object of this improv is to have what seems like a normal conversation, but each actor must use only questions when speaking. Actors can't repeat or rephrase someone else's question. If an actor says a statement, he is disqualified.

Remind the students that questions start with words like: why, where, who, how, did, are, and is. The teacher should act as the referee, making sure that the questions make sense and follow the rules. This improv can be done by two or more actors. In the two actor version, if one of the actors makes a mistake, he may be replaced by a teammate waiting in the wings. If that team uses up all of its members, the other team wins. It can also be done with several actors as an elimination game with the last two remaining declared the winners.

64. Change the Object

Needed for this improv are some objects that can become many things in the imaginations of the students. I suggest a yardstick, a large bath towel or piece of fabric, some bendable wire, a four foot piece of rope, a ball, and anything else unusual in shape.

Divide the students into teams. The teacher picks which object to start with and each team takes turns using the object in an original way. For example, the yardstick can become a clarinet, a baseball bat, a telescope, etc. The students don't just say what it is, they must show it by using the object. The more clear the mime, the better. The students may use partners from their team if support is needed. The team with the most ideas wins the round for that object and the team winning the most rounds wins the game.

65. Slide Show

This improv needs two students to act as Narrators and four other students to be the pictures or slides. The usual starting situation is a viewing of vacation slides. The audience or the teacher picks the countries visited. The two Narrators briefly explain how thrilled they are to have a chance to show off pictures from their trip to the audience. They mention which country they want to show first and can give hints to the students serving as the pictures. For example, "Here's a shot of a chicken-plucking festival," or "These are some local entertainers doing a dance performance."

The Narrators then say, "click, click" and the students acting as the slides begin to move in unusual positions. When the Narrators say "click, click" again, the slide freezes and one or both of the Narrators explain what that slide is about. It's funniest when they come up with something unexpected, not at all what the slide may look like.

Situations
Dating lessons
Animal slides
How to win at video games
Cell phone photos of people in strange situations

66. Emotional Symphony

This improv is good for warming up the voice with a little silliness thrown in for good measure.

A list of emotions is posted on the board — happiness, surprise, boredom, disgust, stupidity, sorrow, anger, confusion, love, conceit, frustration, etc., — and one or two students volunteer to present an emotion. This can be done with just sounds and gestures, or with words. Half the students line up across the front of the room and a Conductor is chosen to lead the symphony. The Conductor's first job is to check the tuning of each emotion, giving the audience a brief sample of the sound. The Conductor can then pick sounds at random, have two or more going at the same time, or increase and decrease the volume. It's best to end with all of the sounds going at once, and then cut off to total silence with a final solo by one of the more interesting emotions. The Conductor then encourages the audience to applaud the musicians and then the musicians all applaud the Conductor as he takes his bow.

67. Foreign Expert

This improv is a variation of Slide Show. It uses the same two Narrators and four students to act out the slides, but the scene features the addition of an Expert from a foreign country who speaks no English. The Narrators welcome the Expert and explain what topic he's come to speak about with accompanying slides. They can even take questions from the audience that they must translate for the Expert. The foreign language is just gibberish. When the Expert answers questions or explains the slides, the Narrators translate what he says. Basically, the pressure is all on the Narrators. They must be imaginative and able to think quickly off the top of their heads.

68. Putting in a Good Word

This improv should be demonstrated by the teacher first, so the students can see how it is done. Explain to the students that you will be making up a short speech, extemporaneous speaking, and as you go along you will point to various students who must shout out a word that you will incorporate into your speech. Remind them that only *appropriate words* will be considered. The teacher can pick from the list of topics below, make up his own topic, or get input from the class on suggested topics for this short speech.

Remember, you don't have to use the word you're given right away. You can set yourself up first and find an unusual approach to the word. Be sure to stay within your original topic and do not wander. Don't let the words push you around. After demonstrating for the students, allow volunteers to give it a try. Remember, it's always best to stop them when things are going well. Don't let it go on too long or fizzle out.

Topics

Things a person can do to avoid doing homework
Good excuses for missing work
Places in the world I have never traveled to and why
The fine art of eating and my favorite foods
What it would be like if students ran the school
Fun jobs and awful jobs
How to look on the bright side in every situation
The problems one might encounter having various zoo animals for pets
Fun things to do on a rainy day
A day at the mall
How to train your parents
Beach safety
How to avoid getting into fights on the playground

69. Life Sports

This improv is for three students. One is the Competitor, one is the play-by-play Sportscaster, and one is the Background Sportscaster.

The Competitor is assigned some simple task to act out, bearing in mind that even if it's just brushing one's teeth, it must be done with the flair of a professional athlete in an intense competition, like the Olympics. As the scene progresses, the Sportscaster follows and comments on what the Competitor is doing at the moment, while the Background Sportscaster interjects made-up bits of history about the Competitor's life, training methods, and past successes.

70. Party People

This improv tests students' powers of observation.

One or two students are chosen as Hosts for the party scene. Three others are chosen to be Party Guests. The Hosts momentarily leave the room or enter the cone of silence while the class decides what attributes, personality quirks, or strange behavior will be demonstrated by each Party Guest. It's the Hosts' job to correctly identify each Party Guest's peculiarity.

71. Lines, Please

This improv has no script, but there are *lines*. In this two- or three-person scene, each actor is given two cards with lines or phrases on them that he must read some time during the scene and try to make it fit the situation.

Sample lines:
That's funny, you don't seem like that type to me.
I'm in a great deal of pain.
I guess you're darned if you do, and darned if you don't.
Someone should call the police!
I can't believe I'm doing this.
I don't want to hear another word.
Could you repeat that? All of it?
Did I hear what I think I heard?
It's so romantic, isn't it?
This could be dangerous.
You think I'm to blame, don't you?
When you're dead, you're dead.
If only Grandpa could see you now.
Why are you looking at me like that?
If you're so smart, you think of something.
I have a confession to make.
Do I embarrass you?
How do I know you're really my friend?
Homework is not an option.
There's got to be a better way.
That's easy for you to say.

72. Foreign Restaurant

This improv shows that communication can still take place, even if one of the people isn't speaking English.

Two students are selected to act out a scene about ordering food in a foreign restaurant. The person ordering speaks English and the Waiter speaks a foreign language. If the student doesn't speak another language, gibberish is fun too.

In order for the English-speaking person to place his order, he may have to resort to pantomime, wild gestures, charades, or drawing pictures.

73. Fame

One student is chosen to be the Famous Person for this improv. They have to step outside the classroom or into the cone of silence while the class picks a famous person to be interviewed in this press conference scene.

A group of Reporters is chosen and they must ask questions with subtle hints so that the Famous Person can figure out who they are. Remind the students that the fun is in confusing the Famous Person, not giving it away too soon.

74. Talk or Die

This improv teaches the students to really listen to what someone is saying.

Three students are picked to tell a story together. Another student is picked to be the Pointer, who points at one student at a time. The three actors must keep speaking about a topic chosen by the audience until the Pointer points to another student. The Pointer can switch storytellers mid-word. If the new speaker isn't paying close attention, the Pointer and the audience shout, "die." Then the actor who messed up must perform a brief death scene of his own choosing: jumping off a cliff, drinking poison, running out into traffic. There are three ways to mess up: pause too long, repeat something already said, or go totally off the track.

75. One Voice

This improv teaches listening skills and cooperation.

Three students are chosen to tell a story on a topic chosen by the teacher or class. The trick to this improv is that they must all three speak in unison. One trick is to have the center person tap his partners on the back when it's their turn to lead the story.

76. Freeze Frame Finish

This improv involves problem solving.

Two or three students are chosen to act out a scene that will end with them in a particular sculpted pose. To begin, a student is chosen as Sculptor who positions the actors in a frozen tableau — these are the positions the actors must end in. The actors are then given scene suggestions by the audience or teacher. As they go along, they must problem-solve how they will end up in that final tableau.

77. Easy as A-B-C

This improv is good for vocabulary skills such as word choice.

Two or three actors are chosen to act out a scene on a topic chosen by the audience or the teacher. The trick is each new sentence spoken by the actors must begin with progressing letters of the alphabet.

Example of a scene about going to the movies:
STUDENT 1: All of us should go see a movie.
STUDENT 2: Better pick a day we're all free.
STUDENT 3: Can you stay out late?
STUDENT 1: Do you have to go late at night?
STUDENT 2: Each of us gets to suggest a movie we'd like to see.
STUDENT 3: Friday the Thirteenth!
STUDENT 1: Gosh, that's a scary one.

78. Building That Character

In this improv, one student is chosen to have his character created by others who will pass through the scene.

Begin with a simple activity such as typing or making a sandwich. As others are chosen to enter the scene, they provide the first actor with information about his character. For example, the first person to enter might say, "Dad, you sure are up late." The actor now knows to portray an adult. The next to enter might say, "How's that sore back of yours, Dad?" He must now be changed by this new information throughout the scene. The next to enter might say, "Honey, can you warm up a bottle of milk for the baby?" Now he's got work to do. It's probably a good idea to have the students whisper to the teacher what they're going to say before they enter the scene in case the teacher has to censor things.

79. Math Speak

In this improv, the actors are given a situation to act out, but can speak using only numbers. Mood and ideas must be communicated through tone of voice and gestures.

80. Where You Stay?

This improv for two to four actors involves showing the audience that they are in a particular environment. This is done not only by what they say, but by body language and using things in that environment — mimed objects.

Environments

An attic	A garage	A dining room
A church	A fancy restaurant	A bus
A beach	A farm	The mall
A kitchen	A desert	A racetrack
A parade	A rainforest	A plane
A supermarket	A doctor's office	A mountain top
A sailboat	A cruise ship	A highway
A cemetery	Garbage dump	The North Pole
A dance	A castle	The principal's office
A submarine	A hot air balloon	The White House
Post Office	A library	A movie theatre

81. Job Interview

This improv can help students prepare for the world of work through practicing mock job interviews.

The teacher can conduct the interview or have students play that role, giving them a list of questions for the applicant. The students can pick the kind of job they'd like to interview for or it can be chosen at random from suggestions in a hat.

Interview Questions

What qualities do you have that will help you to succeed in working for us?

What salary range are you hoping for?

What days and what kinds of hours are you available?

What are your strengths and weaknesses?

What are some of your accomplishments?

82. Read and Remember

After reading a selection of any class content, ask the students to partner up and discuss what they remember about the piece. The teacher walks around the class observing the discussions and picks one or two pairs to perform their conversation with the whole class watching, thus reinforcing the points from the content for all.

83. Emotional Roller Coaster

This improv is for two or three actors at a time. Given a situation to act out during the scene, each actor must transition from a starting emotion to an ending emotion. The change should be gradual but can be abrupt if motivated by something that happens in the scene. The audience should be aware of each actor's two emotions from the start of the scene and can be involved in helping to pick the emotions. It sometimes helps to write the actor's name and emotion transition on the board for all to see.

Emotional Transitions
Love to hate
Anger to joy
Joy to sorrow
Love to jealousy
Sorrow to hate

84. Whachu Talkin' 'Bout?

For this improv, partners are chosen and secretly given a topic to discuss in a scene. The focus of the scene is for the two actors to discuss the topic but not give it away. They should make true statements, but not give so much information as to make it obvious what they are discussing. When the teacher calls, "end of scene," the rest of the class tries to guess the topic.

85. Inspired Scene

The teacher or students choose a photograph or a magazine or newspaper article to inspire a scene. This can also be a fun way to present a book report by showing a scene from the book. Students can also create alternative endings for short stories they read in class. History teachers can use dramatizations for current events or historical scenes.

86. Change Is Good

In these two-person scenes, the students act out a given scene, changing their positions as often as possible without getting ridiculous. They should try different walks, leaning, different levels, and ways of sitting or standing. Variety of movement is the goal.

87. Chew Gum and Walk

Students work in partners. The focus of the exercise is for them to do two things at once, such as: eat a meal and break up with a boyfriend or girlfriend, dance and mop the floor, row a slave ship while planning an escape, put on makeup and discuss boys through instant messaging, talk on the phone and play a video game, work on a science project and cut a friend's hair.

88. Wordly Wise

This improv is for two to four students. First they're given the situation for a scene. Then they're given a particular adjective that must influence the way the scene develops as well as be mentioned at least three times in the scene in correct context.

Adjective

Fast	Slow	Excited
Bored	Fearful	Angry
Dumb	Confused	Nervous

89. Flashback

This improv requires two pairs of students to act out a suggested scene. The first pair gets the scene started and when the teacher calls, "flashback," the other two provide a scene from the past that shows the first pair in younger days.

90. Spectator Sports

Groups of three to five students act as Spectators watching a specific sporting event. They can call out to the imaginary players and referees. The Spectators determine if they're winning or losing and what's happening on the field or in the pool.

91. Slo-Mo

Two to four students are give a scene suggestion and begin the scene. When they hear the teacher clap, they go into slow motion until they hear the next clap and resume regular speed.

For an advanced exercise, add fast forward and rewind.

92. Move Me

In this two-person improv, one student is chosen as the Leader and the other the Follower. The students are given a suggestion for a scene. The Follower is not to move unless the Leader is moving. The movement should not be random, but motivated by dialogue and conflict.

93. Do You Know the Time?

In this improv involving two to four students, one of them is secretly told a specific time frame for the scene and must communicate it to the others through subtle hints and actions. The teacher can let the audience know ahead of time with a flash card, or leave them guessing as well.

94. Pause Button

This improv can involve two to four students. Given a situation, the students begin a scene. When they hear the teacher say, "pause," they must freeze in position. The teacher may then comment on what has been happening in the scene or offer suggestions about what will happen next. At the call of "play," the action continues until the teacher calls, "end of scene."

95. Double Casting

This improv needs four students divided into pairs. Given a topic, the first pair begins the scene. At the sound of a hand clap from the teacher, the next pair picks up the scene exactly where the first pair left off. They take the scene further until the next clap, when the first group picks it up and takes the scene to a conclusion.

For an advanced version, try simultaneous scenes, but this can be confusing or hard for the audience to watch.

96. That's Heavy

This scene is for two or three students. The teacher whispers to them the name of some heavy object they must move in the scene, but don't let the audience hear. Pick a Guesser from the audience who must identify what object the actors are trying to move. The teacher can end the scene when they guess correctly or have them wait until the scene is over to guess.

Heavy Objects
A car
A refrigerator
A boulder
An outrigger canoe
A fallen tree

97. Houston, We Have a Problem

This is an improv for two to four actors. Given a situation, the actors first play the scene with no obvious conflict or problem. The scene is then repeated with the same actors adding the problem, which could involve such things as losing one's voice, a sneezing fit, the lights go out, a tsunami is on its way, a loose snake, lightning, back pain, or an attack of cockroaches.

98. Monster Meets Monster

From the following list of monsters, pick two and have two students act out a scene portraying a meeting of those two characters. If necessary, give them a situation or conflict.

Monsters

Frankenstein	Mummy	Swamp Thing
Werewolf	Alien	Zombie

99. Joined at the Hip

For this exercise, the teacher may want to bring in some rope to loosely tie the performers together.

Two students are chosen to be twins who are "joined at the hip." Then the teacher gives them a situation to act out. The suggestions should be activities that lend themselves to physicality.

For an advanced game, tell the twins they can speak only when the other twin is speaking. In other words, they speak at the same time but can say different things.

Another advanced option is that the two could be bitter enemies, always arguing but forced to be together and compromise. They can also be in different emotional states suggested by the teacher or their peers.

A third advanced option is they share the same brain, being exactly alike, always agreeing, and complimenting themselves.

Activities

Changing a flat tire
Learning to dance
Cheerleading practice

100. Join on In (Large Group)

For this exercise, it helps if the students know which order to join in, so have the students pick numbers from a hat. The student with the number one is told to come up and mime an activity that could involve a group of people. If they need help with an idea, it's OK for the teacher to whisper a suggestion like planting a garden, lifting weights, or sawing wood.

The student with the number two must figure out what the first student is miming and then join in the activity, preferably doing something different, yet related to the overall theme. For example, if the first student was sawing wood, the second might take the wood from the first and mime nailing it, like they were building a house. Others then join in when it's their turn. When the scene starts to look a little full, a new pantomime is started and the game continues until every student has a chance to participate.

If a student can't think of anything to do, or simply doesn't want to, even after being given a suggestion from the teacher, it should be alright for them to pass. As the teacher, be aware of the difference between not knowing what to do and not wanting to try. Offer encouragement, but don't make participation an issue. The student may need to see how an exercise is done several times before feeling comfortable enough to give it a try.

101. Pick a Card

This exercise requires a little preparation. The teacher, with help from the students, creates three stacks of cards: one stack with cards listing types of people or famous people, one stack listing locations, and the other stack listing a particular activity.

Three students are chosen to improvise a scene. The first picks a *who* card, the next a *where* card, and the last a *what* card. The students can then choose to have sixty seconds to make a plan for the scene, or choose to "go for it" by beginning the scene with no prior planning. Each student should read their card aloud so the audience knows what elements must be covered in the scene.

Suggestions for Who

A movie star	A local entertainer
A famous musician	A TV character
An undertaker	A pilot
A dance instructor	The director of a music video
A parent	A famous politician (living or dead)

Suggestions for Where

Undersea wreck	Cave	Airplane
Space station	Petting zoo	Rock concert

Suggestions for What

Family picnic	Emergency operation
Spy mission	A search for a lost object

102. Talking Objects

Two or three students are chosen to be Talking Objects in a scene. Other students may be chosen to be People in the scene. The students playing the parts of the Talking Objects in the scene should whisper whenever the People are around but may speak freely when they're gone. The Talking Objects may complain about how difficult their life is and how People misuse them, ignore them, or don't appreciate them.

For advanced play, the humans in the scene should move and use the objects.

103. Superheroes

To prepare for the improv, the teacher, with help from the students, comes up with a list of unusual superheroes and a list of problems or some kind of crisis that only a hero can solve.

Three students are chosen to be superheroes. The first is given or selects a superhero name from the list and is assigned a problem to solve. What each superhero says and does to solve the problem must directly relate to his superhero name. For example, Flame Boy would use fire somehow and Talks-Them-to-Death Woman would keep yakking at the villains until they nearly die.

The first superhero sets the scene and gets things rolling, but realizes he needs the help of other superheroes. He summons them to help, picking a name from the list, or making up one of his own. Each superhero who enters acts the way one would suspect considering his namesake. It should take the work of all three heroes together to save the world.

Note: Explain to the students that these scenes are performed in an exaggerated, melodramatic style.

Conflicts

The evil Dr. Do-Bad is aiming a stupidity ray at the nation's capital.

The sinister Master Freeze has frozen the island of Maui and is holding it for ransom.

That no-good mobster Mugsy McFutt has cancelled all flights from Alaska to his Las Vegas casinos and Alaskan residents are going through gambling withdrawal.

The sinister General Ali Ben Bazza and his terrorist army have kidnapped Britney Spears from her USO show.

Ronald Rumbutt, the Secretary of Defense, has become the zombie slave of alien invaders and is threatening to nuke North Dakota for bombing practice.

Superhero Names

Dirty Diaper Boy Wonder
Tickle Girl and her flying fingers of torture
Snot Man and his super snoz-olla
Bad Hair Day Woman and her hairspray death ray
Popsicle Person and his Brain Freeze mind control machine
Lava Woman, too hot to handle
Pothole Man and his sloppy jalopy
Super Shopper Girl and her blazing credit cards
Rock Man with his heavy metal guitar and ear-splitter amp
Goody-Two-Shoes Girl and her homework-filled purse
Wedgie Boy and his underpants of power
Makeup Woman, mistress master of disguise
Know-it-All Man and his amazing memory
Chicken Girl and her atomic eggs
Leads-with-His-Butt Man
Cries-about-Everything Girl and her tears of powerful persuasion
Ghost Boy and his scary howl
Caffeine Kid and his runaway mouth
Loves-to-Lie Woman and her fantastic fibs

104. Scenes from a Hat

To prepare, fill a hat with wacky situations and another hat with suggestions for *one-liners,* short, funny sentences made up by the participants.

Divide the class into two teams. Each team takes turns picking a situation from the hat. Members from each team alternate, with one team member at a time coming stage center to say his funny one-liner relating to the situation. When one of the teams can't come up with any more ideas, or simply presents one that is so bad, so not funny that it makes one groan, then a point is given to the other team and a new suggestion is pulled from the hat. I suggest you keep the game short rather than run it into the ground.

Find ways, like strange rules, to keep the scoring even so it's more exciting for the students.

Suggestions from the Hat

Things you don't want to hear when you finish your last bite of
    dinner
Things they probably put in school lunches but never tell you
Giving your date's parents just a little too much information
Your best excuses for having a late homework assignment

The many ways to waste or lose your money

Things your doctor says that make you suspect that he or she
never finished medical school

What you don't want to read in your fortune cookie

Excuses you rarely hear for speeding in a motor vehicle

Scary movie titles with everyday objects in the title

When cartoon characters go bad

Things you don't want to get for Christmas

The terrible things that can happen to you at summer camp

What would life be like if students had famous people teaching
their subjects at school?

Things you don't want to hear your parents say

Things you're never going to hear your teachers say

Great pick up lines when meeting guys or girls at the mall

The many ways to aggravate your siblings

Things it is best not to say when being questioned by the police

Things you don't want to hear while having an operation

Famous sayings that are misquoted or mixed up

Tattoos you don't want to see on your friends or family

Times when it's best to run as fast as you can

What pets would say if they could talk

Things you don't want to find in your parachute pack

World's worst people to be President of the United States and
what they might do or say

Times when it's not a good idea to break into song

Personal messages you don't want to see flying from the back of
an airplane

The wrong songs to sing in prison

Things parents shouldn't say when trying to build your self-esteem

105. Dating Game Show

A Contestant is chosen to ask questions of the game show's Bachelors or Bachelorettes. But first, the Contestant must enter the cone of silence. While the Contestant is in the cone of silence, three Bachelors or Bachelorettes are chosen and given some unusual characteristic or quirk that the Contestant must guess after asking each potential date two or three questions. The humor in the scene comes from the strange questions the Contestant asks and how each quirk affects the answers.

Quirks

The person is grounded.
The person speaks backwards.
The person is egotistical.
The person is afraid to be alone with anyone of the opposite sex.
The person loses his temper easily.
The person is a clown from the circus.
The person is obsessed with video games.
The person is a psychiatrist who analyzes everything he hears.
The person is a tightwad when it comes to spending money.
The person only wants to do things that involve the ocean.
The person wants every date to help with homework.
The person has severe dietary restrictions.
The person likes to eat constantly.
The person is half dolphin.
The person uses lines from popular songs.
The person is afraid of heights.
The person is obsessed with TV.
The person is a witch or warlock.
The person uses a different voice with each sentence he or she
    speaks.
The person is a bragging stunt person in the movies.
The person is a power-crazy police officer.
The person is a professional wrestler.
The person is a caveman or woman.
The person has lots of secrets.

106. Is That All You Can Say?

For this improv, two or three students are chosen for a scene and given a situation. Then they must each pick two lines from a hat. They can have as many lines of their own as they need to set up the situation for the line from the hat they're about to read.

The focus of the exercise is to try to make those two lines chosen from the hat seem to make sense while following the given situation.

Suggested Lines

Should I be doing this?
Oh, now we're in trouble.
Why do you always do that?
Don't worry, I'm a doctor.
I want to go first.
Is that all you're going to do?

I've never seen anything like it.
This is unbelievable.
You've got to be kidding.
I wouldn't do that if I were you.
We've got to get out of here.
This is all your fault, you know.
Now that I like.
You've got to be crazy.
Are you enjoying this?
Did you hear that?
I know what we've got to do now.
Easy does it.
How are we going to explain this?
You are something else.
Don't tell me what to do.
I've hurt myself.
I need your help.
Why are you looking at me like that?
Don't give up.
I knew you'd say that.
This isn't getting us anywhere.
We've got to work together.
I'm not buying it.
Well, look what we've got here.
This isn't going to work.
Can I trust you?
You like me, don't you?

107. Stylin'

To prepare, the teacher will need to put scene styles in a hat for this exercise.

For this improv, two to four students are chosen and given a situation for a scene. Then one of them picks a scene style from the hat. The students then act out the situation utilizing that particular style.

Styles

Animé	Documentary	Kid's show
Western	Horror Movie	Melodrama
Musical	Cartoon	Kung Fu Movie
Shakespearean	Reality Show	Comedy
Tragedy	Talk Show	Infomercial
Pidgin		

108. Rhymin' Simon

The premise of this improv is simple: no matter what the scene is about, the actors must try to stay on topic, but rhyme every line. They can rhyme with their partner's line or each do couplets. It can be like a rap. The emphasis is on making sense and rhyming.

109. Musical Mimes

This improv involves miming. No spoken words; just gestures, facial expressions, body language. The teacher picks several different kinds of music to play as the underlying score for this scene. The actors should be influenced by the music. The scene can involve one to three actors. Much more and it can get distracting. The students need to learn to share the spotlight and take turns leading the mime. They shouldn't all do different things at the same time, but support one another.

110. Time Travel

This improv involves four actors. The first actor begins a brief scene dealing with a specific time of day, of his own choosing, or from a suggestion by the teacher or class members. After about one minute, the next actor joins him but starts a new scene that takes place at a different time of day. After another minute, a third actor starts a new scene, then a fourth, all in different time frames. Then they exit, one by one, leaving the first actor and his time frame. It's a good memory stretcher to remember what was happening and pick the scenes up where they left off.

111. How Touching

In this improv, the actors may speak only when touching another actor. This sets the stage for discussing proper kinds of touch, but hopefully it won't be a problem. If the students aren't trusted to behave, don't try this one with them. There are plenty of other improvisations to try.

112. People Puppets

Four actors are used in this improv. Two actors are the puppets and two are the puppeteers.

Options:

The puppets can't say a word and the puppeteers do all the talking and moving for them.

The puppets can't talk, but they can help with the movement.

The puppets can talk, but can't move without the assistance of the puppeteers.

113. Life's Entrances and Exits

Two actors begin a scene. A third actor enters, justifying his being necessary to the scene. Then, one of the original scene partners must leave, justifying the reason for his exit. The process can repeat itself with new actors as long as the teacher likes.

114. I Remember When

In this improv, two actors sit on a bench, reminiscing about some past events. Two other actors must then act out that event.

115. Overdubbing

In this improv, two actors supply the voices for two other actors creating the scene. What the voices say can lead the scene, but the other actors' movements and expressions can lead as well.

116. Sound Effects

Actors on-stage play a scene, but must hear and comment on strange sound effects made by selected off-stage voices.

117. Denial

In this improv, no matter what happens in the given scene, one of the actors disputes it, argues against it, and is completely negative. The actors must not let this negativity keep them from advancing the scene.

118. Words, Words

This improv can include numerous actors. The teacher or audience suggests a topic for a story or news report and the chosen actors tell the story, each adding only one word at a time.

For an advanced game, don't have an order of who speaks. Let them work it out.

119. Writer's Block

One actor is chosen to be the scene Writer. The Writer pretends to be typing out a scene, speaking it out loud as he types. When he pauses, other actors come on-stage to act out what the Writer is suggesting. Hopefully, Writers won't have to be reminded not to set others up for embarrassment. They must accept that the teacher can stop a scene at any time if they deem the content inappropriate.

120. First Line, Last Line

In this improv, three actors are selected. They are given a first line and a last line to read aloud. They then have fifteen seconds to come up with a scene that makes sense starting with the line given and ending, not too soon, with the last line given. This encourages quick thinking and cooperation.

121. Movie Director's Editing Room

In this improv, a group of actors are chosen to be Stars in a movie, and one to be the movie Director. The Director sets up the situation and the Stars do the first scene. At any time, the Director can call out, "Cut to the flashback, five years ago," "Cut to the wedding scene," "Now the big argument," "Cut to the car chase," or anything else the Director chooses. The fun here is in the Stars' ability to switch gears quickly.

122. Props

In this improv, three actors are given three unusual props and must incorporate them into a given scene.

123. In a ... With a ... While a ...

The audience or teacher gives suggestions for a scene with three actors. The first actor shows where the scene is happening, *in a,* the next person comments about the object, *with a,* and the last person concentrates on the conflict, *while a.* For example: *In a* jungle *with a* monkey *while a* commercial is being filmed.

124. Sell It

This improv is about acting in commercials and the tricks of advertising. One or two actors at a time are auditioning to sell a product, real or made up. They can use such tricks as: appealing to experts, "Four out of five doctors agree ... "; star appeal, "I'm Jessica Simpson and I use Pits deodorant"; comedy; the warm and fuzzy, "Aren't puppies cute? Well, Fresh Air Conditioner can bring that puppy smell to your home."

125. Talk Show

This improv is for two actors. One is the talk show Host and the other is a Guest who can be somebody famous or someone who has been through some unusual life experiences. The talk show Host can make up things about the Guest as well as ask them questions.

Assessing Drama Performance Grading Sheet

Preparation
3 points: The scene is well prepared and the lines are learned.
For improv, the student followed the guidelines and added to the scene.
2 points: Some lines are not memorized.
For improv, the student followed the guidelines but added little to help the scene.
1 point: The student is totally dependent on the script.
For improv, the student did not seem to understand and follow the guidelines.

Projection
3 points: Sufficient volume to be heard by the entire audience.
2 points: Some difficulty being heard.
1 point: Not loud enough.

Pronunciation
3 points: All dialogue spoken clearly.
2 points: Some lines not clear.
1 point: Difficult to understand.

Poise
3 points: Movements and gestures seem natural and support the context of the line or scene.
2 points: Some awkwardness to movements or gestures.
1 point: Nervous fidgeting, or no movement or gestures.

Talent — ability to hold audience interest
3 points: Star quality.
2 points: Interesting to watch.
1 point: Kind of dull.

Total Number of points possible: 15

Scores
15-13: Look out, Hollywood!
12-9: Star potential.
8-5: Don't quit your day job.

Chapter Five
Public Speaking Made Easy

Every time someone speaks in front of a group of people it's a two-way street: the audience's ability to listen, and the message the speaker has for them. It's the job of the audience to be polite, respectful, thoughtful, and kind to the speaker or actors in a play. Because it's live, not recorded like movies or TV, every sound, even the expressions on the faces of the audience, can influence the speaker or the actor. Everyone likes to be listened to and the favor should be returned when the roles switch from speaker to audience member.

There are just a few important things for a person speaking in front of a group to remember:

- Make eye contact with people in the audience and wait until the audience is ready to listen before the speaker begins.
- The audience has got to be able to hear the speaker. The speaker needs to speak loud enough for everyone to understand what is being said, or the audience will get frustrated because they can't hear it all and just stop listening.
- The speaker must speak clearly. That means enunciate. Pronounce each word clearly enough to be understood by the entire audience.
- The speaker needs to vary the way he speaks so it's not boring. Sometimes it's OK to get loud, particularly at the parts the speaker wants to emphasize. At other times it's acceptable to bring the volume down, but not so low the audience can't hear. Silence can work for the speaker, too. A pause in the right spot gets everyone's attention. The speaker can change his pitch, making his voice higher or lower. Doing so makes the speaker's talk more interesting, more engaging for the people listening. Trying other voices or impersonations can also make it fun.
- Don't fidget. Don't fool around. Don't hide, don't lean, and don't apologize. If the speaker likes to move, make every gesture and every step count.

Public Speaking Made Easy
- Wait until the audience is quiet.
- Show confidence and make eye contact.
- Speak loud and clear and give it enough variety to be interesting.
- Don't fidget around and if the speaker does move, make every gesture count.

Now would be a good time to have students demonstrate these points by having some volunteers read a few speeches and poems.

126. Gestures

Without saying a word out loud, have the students use just their arms and hands to say, "Come here." Then try, "You, yes you, should be real quiet." Next try, "It's hot in here."

Other Options
You, come here, now!
Can you give me the time?
Can you speak up?
That's not nice.
You can go.
That person's crazy.
I am so tired.
I'm so hungry.
Something smells.
This is giving me a headache.
You're in trouble.
Want to fight?
I'm watching you.
He's crazy.
Shame, shame.
Talk to the hand.
Do you know the time?
Peace.

Guidelines for Public Speaking: The Three Ps

Projection
Speak loud enough so that it can be heard by everyone in the room. If using a microphone to address an assembly, be sure to speak close enough to the microphone for it to pick up the speaker's voice.

Pronunciation
Speak words clearly. Be sure to pronounce the consonants at the end of words. Don't be a mush mouth and don't speak too fast.

Poise

Stand calmly when making a presentation before a class. Don't fidget with clothes. Keep feet on the floor. Don't lean on anything. Look at all the people in the audience. If the speaker is afraid to make eye contact, one trick is to look slightly over their heads. Don't hide behind the paper if using notes.

Other Points to Ponder

Memorize important parts so the speaker won't sound like he is reading. Make the presentation sound interesting. It's OK to use dramatic pauses. If the speaker loses his place, say, "pardon me," find it, then go on. Emphasize important parts by saying the words louder, or repeating a phrase.

Memorization Techniques

When it comes to learning lines, memorizing poems, speeches, or what have you, I am reminded of my drama professor, Dr. Rabby, who said, "Repetition is the mother of skill." There is no substitute, no shortcut that works better than simply repeating the thing that needs to be memorized over and over.

- The speaker should challenge himself to say it four times at least, then take a break. If the piece is large, work on one section at a time. Don't add anything else until the first section is memorized.
- Reading the lines or speech into a tape recorder and listening to it over and over again can help, too. That's how people learn the words to songs they hear: repetition.
- If the speaker has the piece written down, he can cover parts with a card and just learn one line at a time. If he makes a mistake, he goes back to the start. It becomes easier the more he does it.
- The speaker should say it to himself during those everyday moments when he has a little free time. He should keep the script with him so he can refer to it often. Practice saying it to a friend. The more times the speaker says it, the easier it is.

Chapter Six
Monologues and Duologues

127. Old?

This is a monologue for teachers to model for the students.

Let me start off by saying that I know, to you kids, I seem ... well, old. Maybe even *real* old. But I want you to know something ... the kid in you stays young, even though the body goes through lots of changes.

You're probably glad you're young. I wouldn't trade places with you. Not with what I know now. As I've grown older, I've gained new responsibilities, had adventures, learned a bit, met some great people, and avoided some others. I've followed a few dreams, though it seems my dreams keep changing. I appreciate things more, moments like this one.

I mentioned I've learned a bit, and what I've been working on lately is to keep centered. That means sort of watching what I think and wanting to be the best I can be. I'm learning how important choices are. I get excited over creating things: writings, poems, sculpting, watercolors ... I want the list to go on and on.

You see, you do things because you can. It's all about finding out what you can do, isn't it? Now, I bet I've got you wondering what fun things you can look forward to as you ... grow old*er*. You're going to learn to drive and you'll find out how dangerous that can be. My recommendation: It's not a race. The right lane gets you there as good as the fast lane. You can travel the world, and buy stuff like cars and houses and boats and planes ... but all that takes money, so have a plan, or a job. And don't just get any job. Find something you like. And my advice on all of it: Be careful what you want, 'cause you might get it. Because most times, you end up doing what you want to anyway.

People ask me, "Do you get forgetful as you get older?"

Well, you better ...

It's better to forget racism. Negativity. Grudges. Life's too short to dwell on troubles from the past. That's one thing you notice as you get older: No matter how old you get, life's short. Time just seems to go faster with age.

Now, you're all still young, so don't get worried about being old. I'll tell you the secret:

You can still stay as young as you want to be up here *(Points to head.)* Or here. *(Points to heart. Now ask the students if there are any questions and try to answer them remaining in character.)*

128. Tongue-Tied Pirate

In this scene, encourage the audience to repeat after the pirate for some tongue twister fun. This can be a solo piece or split between several actors.

(Enters singing) I was born on a pirate ship, well hold your tongue and don't you slip.

Yes, I was born on a pirate ship and lived to tell the tale.

Let me hear you say, "Arrrrg!" What a pitiful pack of pirates you'd make! Louder! "Arrrrg!" That's better.

Now me tale can be told.

I was shipped out on the boat, The Broken Barnacle ... manned by none other that Captain Pat the Pirate! He was a sword-swaggering swine if I ever saw one. Yes, a sword-swaggering swine. Always shouting out, "Heave to and hoist that rotten riggin'!"

After we got a belly full of that, me and me mates shouted "Mutiny! Mutiny!" And faster than you can shout, "Stand to starboard and point to port," Captain Pat was perched upon the precipice of the plank, yes, perched upon the precipice of the plank. But Captain Pat refused to jump, that lily-livered coward, so the crew shouts, "Throw that overbearing blockhead over board." Now don't you think that surely the sharks delightfully dined on that dear old captain of mine?

Thank you, I had a nice time.

129. Shake-Speared

This is made up of famous lines from many of Shakespeare's plays, but can seem like a scene in itself. It may be confusing, but it can also lead to a discussion about Shakespeare's plays and his writing style.

Ah, the play's the thing.

This poor player who struts and frets
his hour upon the stage
and then is heard signifying nothing
Friends! Romans! Countrymen!
The quality of mercy is not strained

Not by the stings and arrows
of outrageous fortune.

And who knows not
where a wasp wears its tail?

A tale told by an idiot
Full of sound and fury,
Now that is a question.

Whether 'tis nobler to bury Caesar
Than to praise him
Tomorrow, and tomorrow, and tomorrow
Creeps in its petty pace from day to day
And all our yesterdays
Are but the hour of our discontent.

Oh, that this too, too solid pound of flesh
Would melt like a glove upon that hand.

Alas, poor Yorick, I knew him well
But Brutus says he was ambitious.

Out, damned spot, I say!
Cowards die many times before their deaths.
Is this a dagger I see before me?
That too is a question.

A horse! A horse!
My kingdom for a horse!

Eyes look your last.
Thus with a kiss, I die.
Alack, alack, alack
Blow wind and wrack
Trippingly on the tongue, I die.

My lord, my Liege
If you prick us, do we not bleed?
I fear to sleep, to dream
To shuffle off this mortal coil
The way to dusty death.

Out, out brief candle.
Parting is such sweet sorrow.
To be, or not to be.

What was the question?

130. What's "Up"?

A crazy monologue for the teacher and a lesson on the complexities of the English language.

Alright, students … listen up. *(Looks up.)* I've got a question for you: What's *up?* I'm not asking how you're doing, I'm asking what do you know about the word *up*. It's got a lot of meanings, I'll tell you that. Leave it to the creators of the English language to take a two letter word and give it a whole bunch of meanings. Let's take a look at that word.

Ask yourself: Why is it, when you awaken each morning, they say you wake up? Aren't you lying down? Then, when you're getting ready for school, you get dressed. But if you get dressed up, that's something special.

Let's just say you dressed like everyone else. All in the same school T-shirt. How come some kids brighten up a room, like you *(Name kid)* and some don't *(Name troublemaker)*?

What does a person want you to do when they say, "Speak up"? Talk to the clouds?

And what about food? First you work up an appetite, then you warm up some leftovers, then you have to eat them all up, and then you have to clean up after yourself. And if the kitchen drain gets stopped up, you gotta open it up. That's a lot of up going on.

English can sure be a confusing language. For example, what do your folks or your teachers tell you to do when you don't know how to spell a word? They say, "Look it up"! You have to know how to spell it to do that!

What a mixed up, messed up language.

Why do you lock up a house and lock down a prison?

Here's two things you kids are good at: stirring up trouble and thinking up excuses. Another thing you young people are good at: calling your friends up on your cell phone. But they're not up, are they? They're over … over there someplace. You call over, not up.

Are there any athletes in the house? Can you explain something to me? What do you do when you "Get up for the game"? What does that mean?

You can open up a store in the morning, close it up at night, close it down if it doesn't make money, but you don't open it down. The whole thing's confusing, I tell you.

It's easy to get mixed up. There's another up.

There's ups all over. Up here. Up there. It just don't add up.

Well, I bet you're starting to get fed up with me. I bet you wish I'd just shut up. So I better wrap things up with that old joke: What's up? The sky. But is it clouding up or clearing up?

I hope I proved my point: English can sure be confusing. It's enough to make you want to just give up.

Well, I see by the clock that my time is up.

Just remember, the next time someone asks you "what's up," you tell them what I told you.

And if you can't remember, make something up.

131. Do I Exist?

Alone in my head, on no one's mind. Do I exist? My name, on pieces of paper, in files, on lists, exists. Pieces of paper exist. I'm a tree falling in a forest. Trees fall to become paper. No one to hear the sound. I don't care, trees exist. Alone in this forest, this room, my head. Saying this, on no one's mind. I don't care, I exist. A word called caring in black ink on white paper. I don't care, I exist. Even if no one hears, I exist. Even if no one cares, I exist. Someone, someday, will care. I hope.

Chapter Seven

Poetry for Performance

132. Understanding Poetry

In relating to poetry,
whether you find it confusing … or not
You must see it and feel it, like a shivering hot.
From the top of one's head, the words tumble down
Crumpled and broken and twisted around.
Some slumping or soaring from tongue to mind's ear
A rhyme is developing, or so I do fear.

Confined to a pattern? That's a waste of good time,
Though darn it, the poem continues to rhyme.
Now, let's have none of that. It's time to be free
And if you're following all this nonsense
you'll undoubtedly be
amused and confused cuz it's all clear as mud
Like a curtained metaphor night that falls with a thud.

So much for symbolism, but keep it in mind
It's not hard to write poems
if you don't try to rhyme.

133. Jabberwocky

by Lewis Carroll, from *Through the Looking-Glass and What Alice Found There*, 1872.

'Twas brillig, and the slithy toves
Did gyre and gimble in the wabe;
All mimsy were the borogoves,
And the mome raths outgrabe.

"Beware the Jabberwock, my son!
The jaws that bite, the claws that catch!
Beware the Jubjub bird, and shun
The frumious Bandersnatch!"
He took his vorpal sword in hand:
Long time the manxome foe he sought —

So rested he by the Tumtum tree,
And stood awhile in thought.
And, as in uffish thought he stood,
The Jabberwock, with eyes of flame,
Came whiffling through the tulgey wood,
And burbled as it came!
One, two! One, two! And through and through
The vorpal blade went snicker-snack!
He left it dead, and with its head
He went galumphing back.

"And, hast thou slain the Jabberwock?
Come to my arms, my beamish boy!
O frabjous day! Callooh! Callay!"
He chortled in his joy.

'Twas brillig, and the slithy toves
Did gyre and gimble in the wabe;
All mimsy were the borogoves,
And the mome raths outgrabe.

134. The Vorpal Snit

Inspired by Louis Carrols' *Jabberwocky*

Once upon a flip flop,
There lived a Vorpal Snit
Who rode a Fransome Goppler
And spoke with words of "glit"
But a fierce and flying "Krunster"
Brought terror to the land
And all the folks of "Frick Frack" said,
"Someone must take a stand!"
"Fear not, you 'pluffer gunkles,'"
Said the fearless "Vorpal Snit"
I shall face that flying "Krunster"
And I'll "glip" it where it "flits"
'Twas a fierce and "noscious" battle,
With fire, and screams, and "slopter"
But victory came at last to the "Vorpal Snit"
Atop his "Fransome Goppler."

135. Flutter-By

I wish I was a butterfly
    And if you ever ask me, "Why?"
I'd say, "I want to flutter by,
        To fly on loving wings."

Yes, to flutter by in frolic flight.
    If wish you may,
        Then wish you might,
            For peace on earth,
  A peace so dear.
        Now look around.
          It's here.

          It's here.

136. What Poets Do

Oh, you know …
It may seem strange
The way I can rearrange words
To say something
Or nothing at all.
Like scrawl on the wall if you will, and still,
The poet is free.
No, I will not be confined by my commentary,
Absolutely unrestrained,
I'm a runaway train
Not a trained little dog in a circus,
Not the least bit bound.
I speak for the sake of sound
Bursting around your ear bones
Like headphones filled with rock and roll.
An imaginary stroll on a tightrope of time
And nonsense and rhyme
Just for you,
Because that's what poets do.

137 What Poets Do — For Four Actors

ALL: Yo!
ACTOR 1: You know, it may seem strange
ACTOR 2: the way
ACTOR 3: we
ACTOR 1: can
ACTOR 4: rearrange
ACTOR 1: words
ACTOR 2: to say something
ACTOR 1: or nothing at all.
ACTOR 3: Like scrawl on the wall, if you will.
ACTOR 4: And still, the poet is free.
ACTOR 1: I will not be confined by my commentary.
ACTOR 2: Not the least bit bound.
ACTOR 1: I speak for the sake of sound.
ACTOR 3: Bursting around your ear bones,
ACTOR 4: like headphones filled with Rock and Roll.
ACTOR 1: An imaginary stroll on a tight rope of time
ACTOR 2: and nonsense
ACTOR 3: and rhyme
ACTOR 4: just for you
ACTOR 1: because that's what poet's do.

138. Thesaurus Poem

by Patience Kanda and Rod Martin

I would be happy … no
                         Cheerful … no
   Delighted to have you by my side
But you're not here.
                   You're absent.
                        You're missing.
I eagerly await your arrival
                   Your entrance
                    Your appearance
But I'm fearfully afraid that you may not show at all
   And then you'll never see my loving loyalty
                And dedicated devotion
And I would be hurt …
               No, wounded
                 No, broken … hearted.

139. Love Sets You Free

Sometime
In your lifetime
Something opens your eyes
To the love
All around you
And you realize
That if it takes a lifetime
Then how lucky you'll be
And you can love those around you.
Yes, love sets you free.

140. Words at Work

Caution,
Words at work
Creating connections
Carved in conscious momentary memory.
Words like freedom
That can valiantly inspire
Start a fire
Or slowly expire
If
Left
Unsaid

141. Communication Situation

Check out this communication situation:

I pose to those this dedication
this cooperation of information and inspiration
which is an indication of the power of transformation
An illustration of articulation
unbound by punctuation

I present a proclamation revelation
for your consideration

"There's an explanation for every destination."

For further clarification and/or interpretation
of this conversation
I leave you with this quotation:

> "May your participation
> in the exploration of further education
> provide sufficient stimulation of your imagination."

142. Betty Sue

Betty Sue of Tuskaloo
Walks along the railroad tracks
That pass through her small town,
Looking down and remembering the young man, Dan,
Who passed through her life,
Her town,
Her love.

He came to build a school
He left to fight a war a world away.

And when came the day
That train brought him back,
As he stood there beside the track
Betty Sue instinctively knew
That the love she once had come to know
Had died in a battle not so long ago

And only a body here remained
To carry around the living pain
Like the lonesome moan of a passing train.

143. Teenager

I'm a hopeless teenager
But I'll make it somehow.
Life is for living
And I'm going to live mine now.

144. Optimism

What does optimism mean?
It means to keep on hopin'
          when others aren't copin'.
To see the beauty around you.
To see the humor in life and to laugh often.
To dream a future, remembering the past, grounded in the present
          moment.
To be the kind of person who looks for the loving thing to do and
          say.
It means staying positively positive.
To keep on going and growing and trying and learning and
          turning the world on its ear.

We need more optimism around here.

145. Human Racing

Seconds race by
Humans race by the time our day is done
                    we fall at the feet of forever,
                    begging for but a few moments more
     'til …
                    Bang goes the gun,
                              Off at a run,
Chasing each moment by racing each moment
                              And it's gone.
                    No time to mourn it.
     From the day you're born it's a contest with time
                              Find the reason, the rhyme
Though you run 'til you ache with each step you take,
                    Desiring it,
                    Expiring it.
Each second you take up
Can never be made up
So cherish your space in the race.

146. Creating

We think we're so great
                        because we create
But wait ...
                                Humpback whales also create
                                                Their songs.

Most human songs are long gone
                                Swallowed by history
            No matter ... the importance is song
                        And getting along
                                Like harmony.
            Would whales wage war under the sea?
                        Wouldn't that be a silly thing
            when it's so much more fun ... to sing.

147. Grown Up

Grown up?
        An impossible feat.
No one ever really grows up.
We're still kids
Playing different games
Still harboring the same fears.
                I've been growing up for years,
                        I wish I could start growing down.
I like those younger games better.

148. What is Truth?

What is truth?

                Who's to say?
Can truth, like man, pass away?

        If the word were carved in stone
                Mountain Big and in a line
                        Doesn't stone wear to dust
                                amid the test of time?

149. River of Lava Light

There's a river of lava light
    That flows from the mountains to the sea
      From Honolulu to Waikiki
  And though it's only streetlights, right …
    Like Pele's fire
       Progress consumes everything
         In its path
  Perhaps we will be known as the creatures
     Who prefer light
       At night

150. Wishes

Don't wish upon a falling star
  Or set your hopes on a heaven far
When love's the key to paradise
  And peace on earth
      Let love suffice.
Some say the world will end in fire
   And some say ice.
Frost said, From what I've tasted of desire
  I hold with those who favor fire
But if it had to perish twice
  I think I know enough of hate
To say that for destruction
  Ice is also great
     And would suffice.

151. Inhale

Every breath,
  Every conscious breath,
    Can be a meditation of sorts.
      Sniffs and snorts of mother air
Which we hardly appreciate
  Until it's not there for a minute or two.
If only our love for each other
    Could become as indispensable
      As air.

152. Sand is More

Sand is more
　　　　Than something that sneaks
　　　　　　　　Into sneakers,
　　　　Is sifted through fingers,
　　　Plastered in castles.
It is a massive amount of water
　　　　　　　　Showing boulders who's boss,
　　　The futile battle of stone to remain together.
It's a highway at low tide,
　　　A moving hill,
　　　　　Jogging path and moldable bed.
　　　Young minds museum playground
It's little chunks of rock, coral, and shells
　　　And other erosion resistant minerals.
It's crunchy in oatmeal,
　　　Palatable on peanut butter and jelly,
　　　　　　　Not so spicy in soup,
But basically, it's all over everything
　　　　　　　　　at the beach
it's amazing
it's where sea kisses earth
union
shifting alliances and illusions
the softest of stone.

153. Walk, Man

　　　　　Summer heat
　　　　　City street,
I boogie bounce by hustle and bustle
　　　And busses and cusses and traffic jam fusses.
Wrapped in my music, security
　　　　　　　　Blanket of sound,
I cruise this town
　　　Dancing and strolling,
　　　　　Rocking and rolling.
No, you can't say a word
　　　　　Not a one would be heard
　　　　　Not a sad city thing
　　　　　　　As I strut like a king
　　　On my musical mountain of sound
　　　　　　Down town.

72

154. Shark Park

Ever take a walk through Shark Park?
Seaweed greenery
On coral kingdom scenery
But beware of visits at dark.

The king of that scene,
Fast swimming and lean,
Has only one thing on his mind:
To hunt, always seek
Something easy to eat.
Now, isn't it past dinner time?

Night strolls could cost you dear.
The kings of Shark Park rule here.

155. Mosquito

Poor little mosquito,
    He's drawn his last breath.
        For he
            Who bites me
                Tastes death.

156. Life's Highway

Life presents us with many paths,
    Intersection decisions
           Roadblock frustrations
    Dead end relationships
        Stoplight procrastinations
           Speeding dreams
Fender bender love affairs
    Down hill illnesses
        And too soon,
           Exits.

157. Never Forget

never forget
no matter how big you've grown
that you began life's journey as a babe
who couldn't have survived alone
and though you speak in learned circles
with the knowledge of your years
your first utterances were babble
punctuated by tears
no matter how self-sufficient you feel
or what others may have told you
just as in your beginning
you still need someone to hold you

158. Most Alone

The loneliest thing
Is waking up
To the same thing you saw
When you went to sleep
And it only has one eye
That cannot see you, you see?
It's your TV.

159. A Broken Heart

A broken heart is like a night with no stars
Or going to the prom with your mom.
It's a shattered window that lets in the cold.
The sound of old love songs
        played through blown out speakers.
It's a guitar with no strings, no song to play.
A pain, like cancer.
A fever everyone fears to touch.
Oh yes, a broken heart can hurt that much.

160. Strawflower Expectations

Crushed
    Like a flower
Pressed
    Between the pages of my own aching.
Shattered
    By the breaking of my hope.
Strawflower expectations
                Having lost their living luster
Dried up
    Finding no comfort from rain-like tears,
        Which don't,
        Which I won't, let flow.
First flower of loving
        Plucked
            Pressed
                Unable to grow.

161. Love Is All

Love is all I have to give you
Love is all I have to give
Love is all I have
Love is all
Love is
You

162. The Poet's Prayer

Now I sit me down to write,
before I go to sleep this night.
If I should die before I wake,
My penmanship's my least mistake.

163. Wire and Water

Wire and water.
Those are the questions.
Why are we here?
What are we suppose to be doing?
What are our chances?
Why are we waiting?

Life's full of questions.
Can be full of love, which is the answer,
The solution.
Forgiveness.
Hope.
Love that brings joy in the giving.

Wire and water.
Why are we here?
To Love.

Water.
What are we waiting for?
Wire.
Why are we so dumb?
In a life too short for hate and hurt.

What are we waiting for?
Today's the day.
The start of all the love you can hold in your heart.
Wire and water.

164. Shout This Poem

I travel at the speed of poetry
      Moving though time.
Free
      To rhyme or ramble.
  I roam about.
    I sing this poem.
      I laugh.
            I shout this poem to the stars.
 Such sweet release,
   A poem for peace
     In this world of ours.

165. Baby's Day

Hey, little one, how was your day?
Too young to crawl, to draw, to play.
What did you do girl, give me the scoop?
"Same as yesterday: eat, sleep, and poop."

Just a few weeks old and cute as a button.
Don't tell me you just lazed around
Not doin' nothing.
Did you learn new things?
Make memories to keep?
"Hard to say when you just
poop, eat, and sleep."

Well, you just keep on growing,
You've got all the time in the world.
We love just to watch you and hold you,
You're such a good girl.
It's a wonderful world
With so many nice people to meet,
But for now little girl
You just poop, sleep, and eat.

Chapter Eight
Plays and Scenes

166. The Gatherers

The Actors and Aliens are listed numerically so that multiple students can be given parts.

ACTOR 1: They came from the space between the stars in search of *doers* from this Earth of ours.

ACTOR 2: Like a shooting star in the dark night's sky, their ship appeared in the twinkling of an eye.

ACTOR 3: They scanned the planet until they found two likely subjects from an island town.

ACTOR 4: Slowly, silently, they bring their ship near.

ACTOR 5: Not a person on Earth knew there was something to fear.

ACTOR 6: In a flash of light, too bright for eyes, Christy and Shawn were beamed aboard and the ship began to rise.

ACTOR 7: The alien cruiser slipped away, accelerating its pace until the earth looked small as a baseball spinning in space.

SHAWN: Are you OK, Christy?

ACTOR 8: Said Shawn, dangling beside her. They were both stuck in a force field like the web of a spider.

CHRISTY: Yes, but I can't seem to move, there's a ringing in my ears, and I get the strange feeling we're not the only ones here.

ALIEN 1:Very observant ...

ACTOR 9: Said a voice in their heads.

ALIEN 2: Now, if you both behave, we'll loosen the threads.

ACTOR 10: The force field fizzled, Christy whispered Shawn's name ...

ACTOR 11: And out of the darkness, the Gatherers came.

ACTOR 12: They looked somewhat human in shape and in size, but their heads were much bigger and so were their eyes.

ACTOR 13: Their lips never moved, but Christy and Shawn could hear what they said as if it echoed inside their heads from a long ways away.

ALIEN 3: We come from an interstellar dimension, something humans can't see.

ALIEN 4: We perform a certain service, it's complicated, but free.

ALIEN 5: We are the Gatherers. You are our *guests.*

ALIEN 6: We've brought you aboard for some scientific tests.

CHRISTY: We won't cooperate. Please turn your ship around. Take us back to our home and beam us right down.

ACTOR 14: A strange sort of laughter began filling the space and the ship shook with a jolt as it sped off through space.
ALIEN 7: You are in no position to tell us what to do.
ACTOR 15: Said the Gatherers, slowly surrounding the two.
ALIEN 8: We're looking for *doers,* slaves, and you two will do fine.
ALIEN 9: We've been studying your planet and scanning your minds.
ALIEN 10: We can clone millions from your DNA. Warriors for battles, musicians to play ...
ALIEN 11: Your clones might make great ... pets, so we won't mistreat you.
ALIEN 12: And if all else fails, we can always eat you.
ALIEN 13: You're just perfect, not too smart nor too dumb.
ALIEN 14: And there's plenty more on Earth, where you two come from.
ALIEN 15: If you prove useful, we'll go back for the others. Mothers, fathers, sisters, brothers. *(CHRISTY cries softly.)*
ALIEN 16: What is that water that leaks from the eye?
SHAWN: Leave her alone, you're making her cry.
ALIEN 17: Take the young male creature down to the test room.
CHRISTY: I'm staying with Shawn!
ALIEN 18: No! You remain here, in the *guest* room.
ACTOR 16: The vision screens shown from the stars out in space and Christy tried to be strong and wiped the tears from her face.
ACTOR 17: Then she noticed an odor, not nasty, but strong.
ACTOR 18: Then she just fell asleep. She wasn't sure for how long.
ACTOR 19: She awoke to see Shawn stepping into the light.
CHRISTY: Shawn, what did they do to you? Are you sure you're alright?
SHAWN: The Gatherers need us, so they treated me well. I didn't feel a thing when they borrowed some cells.
CHRISTY: Where's your old clothes, that outfit's so strange? And you don't seem like yourself, like something has changed.
SHAWN: They explained everything, told me their plan. They're going to save Earth, and I think that they can.
CHRISTY: Save us for what? To be slaves throughout space? Or a midnight snack? That's not saving our race.
SHAWN: But they have the power to travel faster than light. We could cross to lost galaxies. See the most awesome of sights!
CHRISTY: The only sights I want to see are with my family back home, so if you want to go with them, then you go alone.
SHAWN: They're offering the universe, a life without end ...
CHRISTY: Shawn, I miss my family, my home, my friends, and if you go with them, I guess I'll miss you, too. Like, miss the way you crack

me up with all the stupid things you do.

ACTOR 20: Two hearts inside that spaceship hurtling through space were filled with something special, something very human, and the two of them embraced.

ALIEN 19: Such a touching sight. And we thought you two were resting.

ALIEN 20: Alright, Shawn Two, take the girl down to testing.

SHAWN: No, Christy's staying here with me. You can't change a person who knows how to be free.

ALIEN 21: We command you to obey!

ALIEN 22: And you better decide wisely if you want to live another day.

SHAWN: No. I have a heart and mind of my own. Take me apart piece by piece, but leave my friend alone.

ALIEN 23: As you wish …

ACTOR 21: And from out of nowhere came a beam, and Shawn Two turned into vapor as if his life had been a dream.

CHRISTY: I will never serve you. You can't enslave the free. So as you've done to Shawn, you might as well do to me.

ALIEN 24: What kind of reasoning is this that you would rather die?

CHRISTY: I won't give up my freedom.

ACTOR 22: And she began to cry.

ALIEN 25: The experiment has failed. Cast her into space!

ALIEN 26: No. This is something we've never seen in any other race. Dry your tears, earthling, we'll take you both back home.

ALIEN 27: We didn't vaporize your friend, that creature was his clone.

ALIEN 28: If you love your freedom so, what awful slaves you'd be.

ALIEN 29: And that thing you do, called tears, that's quite a mystery.

ACTOR 23: Then Shawn returned and he and Christy embraced. Now both were shedding tears.

ACTOR 24: And the spaceship of the Gatherers sped back across light years.

ACTOR 25: Yes, humans need their freedom to live and learn and grow.

ACTOR 26: And that's how two kids saved our planet. We just thought you'd like to know.

167. The History of the Entire World in Ten ... Minutes

The size of the cast is up to the director. It can be done by as few as five or divided up among an entire class. For lines that need to be by the same actor they have been labeled as ACTOR A.

ACTOR: Ladies and Gents, they said it couldn't be done ...
ACTOR: Shouldn't be done.
ACTOR: But with the help of this fine group of actors ... *(ALL bow.)*
ACTOR: We present the History of the Entire World!
ACTOR: In ten minutes, give or take a few.
ACTOR: First, we go back in time.
ACTOR: Way back. Way, way, way back in time ...
ACTOR: Back to the center of the universe.
ACTOR: The dark, emptiness of space ...
ACTOR: When, *bang! (An actor pops a paper bag.)*
ACTOR: The Big Bang — this colossal explosion happens ...
ACTOR: Countless mega tons of matter and energy streak through space at the speed of light.
ACTOR: Then, over billions of years, stars and galaxies begin to form.
ACTOR: The Milky Way, our own galaxy has over one-hundred-billion stars!
(An actor enters with telescope.)
ACTOR: Wow, do you think there's any intelligent life up there?
ACTOR: Better to ask, "Is there any down here?"
ACTOR: Sorry to interrupt, but we've got to hurry.
ACTOR: We'll have to skip over the Paleozoic era.
ACTOR: And the Mesozoic, Cenozoic, and Jurassic eras.
ACTOR: But what about the dinosaurs?
ACTOR: No, we move on to Neanderthal man.
ACTOR: He has a low forehead and small brain.
ACTOR: Remind you of anyone you know?
ACTOR: He was followed by Homo erectus.
ACTOR: And we're not going there ...
ACTOR: And then came us: Homo sapiens, which means *knowing man.*
ACTOR: We began as hunter-gatherers.
ACTOR: If you wanted to eat, there were no fast food restaurants, just fast food.
ACTOR: Catch it, kill it, and grill it. Yum.
ACTOR: We're smart, sometimes...
ACTOR: We adapt, make tools, clothing, shelters.

ACTOR: Early civilizations lived near water.

ACTOR: Surf's up!

ACTOR: Because it attracted animals.

ACTOR: We learned to grow grain,

ACTOR: Settled down into villages,

ACTOR: And as our brains grew, we started doing more thinking.

ACTOR: Even started thinking about thinking, which was the start of Philosophy.

ACTOR: Well, what do you think?

ACTOR: I think there are two types of people. Those who divide people into two types, and those who don't.

ACTOR: Well, everybody is somebody else's nut case.

ACTOR: You know, if people listened to themselves more, they might speak less.

ACTOR: Silence is golden.

ACTOR: But the history of mankind is more than what he *thinks.*

ACTOR: It's about what he *does.*

ACTOR: History books often overlook mankind's greatest ideas and creations, focusing on conflicts and war.

ACTOR: The Trojan war.

ACTOR: The fall of Rome.

ACTOR: The Crusades.

ACTOR: The Revolutionary War.

ACTOR: A Civil War.

ACTOR: World War One: The war to end all wars.

ACTOR: Followed by World War Two.

ACTOR: And three …

ACTOR: Not yet.

ACTOR: There's still those smaller wars: Korea, Vietnam, and the Gulf War.

ACTOR: And don't forget the new gulf war, too. Thank you, George W.

ACTOR: War changes over time like everything else.

ACTOR: It started with rock throwing. *(Actors dressed like CAVEMEN face Off-stage and one throws a sponge rock.)*

ACTOR: Join the club. *(The CAVEMAN that got hit Off-stage with the rock enters and whacks the other one over the head with a foam bat.)*

ACTOR: Armor worked for a while.

ACTOR: *(KNIGHT enters in cardboard box armor.)* Where's the restroom in this thing?

ACTOR: But when bullets came along … *(KNIGHT is shot right in the armor.)*

ACTOR: Then came cannons.

ACTOR: Ka-boom!

ACTOR: Battleships.

ACTOR: Ahoy!

ACTOR: Fighter planes. *(Machine gun sounds)*

ACTOR: Smart bombs.

ACTOR: Like, dir.

ACTOR: Rockets.

ACTOR: We have lift off.

ACTOR: Satellite imaging.

ACTOR: Dude, I can see your house.

ACTOR: Nuclear weapons.

ACTOR: In the event of an attack, crawl under your desk, and kiss your butt good-bye.

ACTOR: War. Dangerous stuff and it's influenced by politics.

ACTOR: We should take a look at government.

ACTOR: Why not, they could be watching us.

ACTOR: And government certainly has a history.

ACTOR: A glorious occupation, where it's best to be sincere, even if you have to fake it.

ACTOR A: Should I run for office?

ACTOR: Why not? A fool and his money are soon elected.

ACTOR: Washington D.C. The land of lobbyists, fringe benefits, and filibusters.

ACTOR A: If elected, I will prove that nothing is often a good thing to do and always a smart thing to say.

ACTOR: Which party are you with?

ACTOR A: Oh, I don't plan to party until I get elected.

ACTOR: Well, if you can't convince 'em, confuse 'em.

ACTOR: Have you picked a theme song for your campaign?

ACTOR A: Yes, this goes out to all my homies out there ...

Call me Fat Cat yea, I hate to rap.
I think that city slicker slop
just sounds so whack.
You grab a massive ghetto blaster
and a microphone.
Do that dance thing with some
Bling bling talkin' on the phone.
Now don't sing it, if you wing it.
Hey, that bothers me.
Mutilate the language
Call that poetry?

Can you do more than rap?

Well, bless my soul.

Raps for them, what can't rock and roll, baby.

ACTOR: So there's a bit of history for you.

ACTOR: Time?

ACTOR: Under ten minutes. *Yes!*

ACTOR: But what about the future?

ACTOR: That's in our hands.

168. Alphabet Soup

A play for middle school actors to perform at elementary schools. The size of the cast depends on the director's preference. For lines that need to be by the same actor they have been labeled as ACTOR A, ACTOR B, ACTOR C, and so on.

ACTOR: This show is about words.

ACTOR: And the alphabet.

ACTOR: Which makes up words.

ACTOR: Words are one of the things that make us humans special.

ACTOR: They help us to say what we're thinking.

ACTOR: And how we feel inside.

ACTOR: Words are how we describe our world.

ACTOR: Like, you're not just a good audience …

ACTOR: You're a great audience!

ACTOR: Marvelous!

ACTOR: Wonderful!

ACTOR: Eh … not bad.

ACTOR: So cool.

ACTOR: So let's begin.

ACTOR: Let's go right through the alphabet.

(ACTOR B starts humming the alphabet song.)

ACTOR: From A to Z.

ACTOR: That should be fun.

ACTOR: Hey, what are you doing?

ACTOR A: Singing the song to myself.

ACTOR: What song?

ACTOR A: The alphabet song. It's the only way I can keep the order straight.

ACTOR: Do you kids know the alphabet song?

ACTOR: Could you sing it with us?

ACTOR: Great. Here we go …

ALL: A-B-C-D-E-F-G, H-I-J-K-L-M-N-O-P, Q-R-S, T-U-V, W, X, Y and Z.

Now I know my A-B-Cs, thank you cuz you sang with me.

ACTOR: They did great!

ACTOR: So, what's the first letter?

ACTOR: Duh …

ACTOR: Duh's the first letter?

ACTOR: No, A.

ACTOR: No way what?

ACTOR: A!

ACTOR: Hey yourself. You lookin' for trouble?

ACTOR: A is the first letter of the alphabet.

ACTOR: And everyone knows that A stands for apple. *(Takes a big bite then talks with a mouthful.)* And it is delicious.

ACTOR: *(Grabs the apple, takes a bite, and speaks with mouth full.)* Lots of words start with A.

ACTOR: Like airplane.

ACTOR: And acrobat. *(Goes into a handstand or does a cartwheel.)*

ACTOR B: I shall now stand on just one finger. Just one. *(Holds up one finger.)*

ACTOR: Nothing to it. *(Takes ACTOR B's finger, places it on the floor, and steps on it.)*

ACTOR B: Ouch.

ACTOR: A is for all. All of us. We're all here now, together.

ACTOR: And in the bigger picture, we're all in this together.

ACTOR C: Huh?

ACTOR: We all make up this wild and wacky world.

ACTOR C: Oh, I see.

ACTOR: No, C, is the third letter of the alphabet. The second letter is B.

ACTOR: And B stands for bad. Some things are good. And some things are bad.

ACTOR: Like the taste of bananas. *(Takes a bite of a banana and with mouth full says)* Good.

ACTOR: Spoiled food. *(Spits.)* Bad.

ACTOR: Chicken … ooooh good.

ACTOR: Chicken Pox, bad.

ACTOR: Hi, I'm on my school's cheerleading squad. I need everyone's help to do a cheer for the letter B. Will you guys help me? OK. *(Cheering style)* Give me a B. Now give me another B. Give me a B. Now give me another B. Give me a B. Now give me another B. Now what's that spell? *(ALL blow a raspberry with fingers to their lips.)*

ACTOR: We need the letter B to spell lots of words.

ACTOR: Yeah, without the letter B, our boats would be oats.

ACTOR: Our beats would be eats.

ACTOR D: Did someone say eat? There's blueberries, and bananas, beans, beef, bacon, bread, butterfish, biscuits, bagels —

ACTOR: OK, OK!

ACTOR D: Brussels sprouts, bubble gum, broccoli, bologna —

ACTOR: Enough already, you're making me hungry. *(Asks the audience)* What letter's next?

ACTOR: C?

ACTOR: And what starts with the letter C?

ACTOR D: Oh, that's easy. Chocolate. And cookies. And candy! *(Throws some candy into the audience.)*

ACTOR: OK, OK, you made your point.

ACTOR D: But there's more. There's chips and chicken, coconuts and cranberries, cabbage and caviar —

ACTOR: OK, OK.

ACTOR D: Cheese and cherries, cucumbers and cauliflower —

ACTOR: Enough.

ACTOR D: Corn and crackers — whoa ... *(Pushed Off-stage, as exiting)* Crab meat and cheesecake ...

ACTOR: Finally, a little peace and quiet.

ACTOR: Now, just calm down.

ACTOR: Calm starts with C.

ACTOR E: Yes, and when you need to feel calm, just take a few deep breaths and you start to relax. *(Breathes too fast.)*

ACTOR: Slow, deep breaths. That's it. Feel better?

ACTOR E: Yes. What's the next letter?

ACTOR: D.

ACTOR D: *(Jumps On-stage with a doughnut.)* Doughnuts!

ACTOR: Out! Out! *(Chases Off-stage.)*

ACTOR: I think she's obsessed with food.

ACTOR: Duh.

ACTOR: Yes, duh starts with D.

ACTOR: And so does dog.

> *(ALL start acting like dogs. Scratching, chasing each other, jumping up, and licking.)*

ACTOR: Help! Sit, boy.

ACTOR: The next letter is E.

ACTOR: Oh, that's an easy one.

ACTOR: E stands for *everything!*

ACTOR: It stands for eagles.

ACTOR: And eternity.

ACTOR D: *(Enters.)* And eating!

ACTOR: It stands for energy, which we young people have a lot of.

ACTOR D: Let's see, I can eat eggs and bacon.

ACTOR: It stands for ears or so I hear.

ACTOR D: Or eggs and spam.

ACTOR: It stands for Earth, the third planet from the sun and the home to everyone.

ACTOR D: Or eggs and rice.

ACTOR: It stands for Echo.

ACTOR: Echo?

ACTOR: Echo!

ACTOR D: Or eggs and sausage.

ACTOR: It stands for electricity, which can be quite shocking.

ACTOR D: Or eggs and toast.

ACTOR: It stands for embrace. Hug me!

ACTOR D: Then there's eggnog at Christmas.

ACTOR: And it stands for equality as in: all men

ACTOR: And women

ACTOR: Are created equal.

ACTOR D: Or eggplant, which is a vegetable, and it's always good to eat your vegetables.

ACTOR: It stands for excited! Oh, boy. Oh, boy. Oh, boy.

ACTOR: It stands for eyes, elbows, earlobes.

ACTOR D: And egg rolls.

ACTOR: Enough already!

ACTOR: Enough starts with E.

ACTOR: That's the end!

ACTOR: End starts with E.

ACTOR: What's the next letter kids?

ACTOR: F. That's right.

ACTOR: And what does F stand for?

ACTOR: I forget.

ACTOR: Yes, forget starts with F.

ACTOR: And so does fashion.

ACTOR: And football. Go long! Go long! Look out! *(The pass receiver hits the edge of the stage.)*

ACTOR: Flat face Freddy, football's fearless fielder.

ACTOR F: F also stands for something very important. I'm talking about ...

ACTOR D: Food!

ACTOR F: No.

ACTOR D: Oh yeah. You got your fish and French fries, fajitas and fried rice, French toast and fruit punch.

ACTOR: F No, I'm talking about freedom.

ACTOR D: Can you eat that?

ACTOR F: No, it's not something you eat. It's something you have.

ACTOR D: Is it contagious? Like the measles?

ACTOR F: No, silly. You see, we live in America, the land of the free.

ALL: *(Singing)* God bless America, land that I love. Stand beside her, and guide her, through the night with the light from a bulb.

ACTOR D: I've heard there's no such thing as a free lunch.

ACTOR F: That's not the kind of *free* I'm talking about. For example, we're free to live anywhere in the country that we like.

ACTOR G: Except Alaska.

ACTOR F: What?

ACTOR G: It's too cold. I could freeze my fanny off. Hey, freeze my fanny, there's two Fs for you.

ACTOR F: But you are free to go there if you like.

ACTOR G: I don't think so. Mom says I have to be home by dark.

ACTOR: There are other kinds of freedom. Like freedom of speech.

ACTOR: What's that mean?

ACTOR: It's means you can say what you like.

ACTOR: You know, you're kinda cute.

ACTOR: Ah, gee …

ACTOR: You're right. The next letter is G.

ACTOR: G is for good. As we said before, there's good and there's bad.

ACTOR: Being kind, good.

ACTOR: Telling lies, bad.

ACTOR: Sharing, good.

ACTOR: Stealing, bad.

ACTOR: I don't get it. I just don't get this whole good and bad thing.

ACTOR H: Allow me to explain. Let's say you win a free plane trip to Maui.

ACTOR: That's good!

ACTOR H: But on the way there, the plane has engine trouble.

ACTOR: That's bad.

ACTOR H: So you put on your parachute and jump out.

ACTOR: That's good.

ACTOR H: But the parachute won't open.

ACTOR: That's bad.

ACTOR H: But luckily, the inter-island barge is coming back from Molokai with a big load of hay and it's right under you.

ACTOR: That's good.

ACTOR H: But there's a sharp pointy pitchfork in the middle of the haystack.

ACTOR: That's bad.

ACTOR H: Fortunately, you miss the pitchfork.

ACTOR: That's good.

ACTOR H: Unfortunately, you miss the haystack. I hope you can swim.

ACTOR: So what else can the letter G stand for?

ACTOR D: Guava juice and graham crackers, guacamole and grapefruit, granola bars and gummy bears, green beans, green peas, green onion, and green grapes!

ACTOR: Is food all you ever think about?

ACTOR D: No! Sometimes I think I have to go to the bathroom. Bye. *(Exits.)*

ACTOR: Have you got a tongue twister for the letter G?

ACTOR I: Sure. Greta grabbed great green gobs of greasy, grimy gopher guts.

ACTOR: Ooooo, gross.

ACTOR I: It's a gift.

ACTOR: OK, kids, what letter follows G?

ACTOR: H! That's right. And what starts with an H?

ACTOR: H is for honeydew.

ACTOR: The melon?

ACTOR: The girlfriend.

ACTOR: You have a honeydew?

ACTOR: Yeah, all the time. She says, "Honey, do dis, and honey, do dat."

ACTOR J: I know another H word.

ACTOR: What is it?

ACTOR J: It's real important.

ACTOR: Is it hopscotch?

ACTOR J: Nope. I'll give you a hint. If you don't have this, you won't feel very good.

ACTOR: Is it happiness?

ACTOR J: No, but it helps us to be happy. Give up?

ACTOR: Yep.

ACTOR J: It's your health. And what can you do to stay healthy?

ACTOR: Eat good food?

ACTOR J: Right.

ACTOR D: *(Enters.)* Did I hear someone say eat? How about hot dogs with hash browns? Or hamburgers with horseradish? Or hot wings with hot fudge?

ACTOR: It's important to eat healthy foods, and not eat too much.

ACTOR: Oh, I know what else helps you to be healthy.

ACTOR: What?

ACTOR: Exercise!

(ALL demonstrate kinds of exercise.)

ACTOR: Aerobics.

ACTOR: Jogging.

ACTOR: Sports.

ACTOR: Hiking.

ACTOR: Swimming.

ACTOR: Paddling.

ACTOR K: OK, OK, you guys. Another thing that helps us to be happy is having a good outlook.

ACTOR: Look out! *(Ducks.)* You said look out.

ACTOR K: I said outlook. That's your attitude. How you think about things. Do you look on the bright side? Can you handle stress? Do you know how to relax? Hey, wake up!

ACTOR: Time for our next letter.

ACTOR: The next letter is I. And luckily, I can't think of a single food that starts with I.

ACTOR D: I can. Ice cream! I scream. You scream. We all scream for ice cream!

ACTOR L: OK, thank you very much. *(Pushing ACTOR Off-stage)*

ACTOR D: And there's shaved ice.

ACTOR L: That's enough.

ACTOR D: And icicles.

ACTOR L: Good-bye.

ACTOR: I is for imagination.

ACTOR: Our imagination is a wonderful gift.

ACTOR: We use it every time we play.

ACTOR: Or create artwork.

ACTOR: Or make up stories.

ACTOR: Oh, I love stories.

ACTOR: OK, kids, what letter follows I?

ACTOR: That's right, J.

ACTOR: And what starts with the letter J?

ACTOR M: Jokes. And I've got a few for you. Ready? Knock, knock.

ACTOR N: Who's there?

ACTOR M: Matthew.

ACTOR N: Matthew who?

ACTOR M: *(With a lisp)* My shoe lace is untied. Knock, knock.

ACTOR N: There's more?

ACTOR M: Yea, knock, knock.

ACTOR N: Now who?

ACTOR M: Ben.

ACTOR N: Ben who?

ACTOR M: Bend over and help me tie my shoelace, please.

ACTOR N: OK.

ACTOR M: Knock, knock?

ACTOR N: Who's there?!

ACTOR M: USA.

ACTOR N: USA who?

ACTOR M: You is a nice person for helping me tie my shoe.

ACTOR D: *(Enters.)* Let's see ... J could be for juice, or jelly beans, jam, and junk food. Oh, man, I love that junk food.

ACTOR: That's not eating healthy, remember?

ACTOR D: But what if I didn't have soda pop, and candy, and Twinkies, and bubble gum?

ACTOR: Then you'd have less cavities.

ACTOR D: Oh.

ACTOR: OK?

ACTOR D: K-den.

ACTOR: Speaking of K, that's the next letter.

ACTOR: K is for kindness

ACTOR: And kisses. *(Blows a kiss.)*

ACTOR O: Ah, shucks.

ACTOR: Take it easy, Romeo.

ACTOR O: Is it time for my big scene?

ACTOR: Not yet, we'll let you know, lover boy.

ACTOR: Ah, love. The L word.

ACTOR: Yes, L can stand for love.

ACTOR: Ah, love. Larry looked longingly at Lisa from London.

ACTOR: Love is one of the best things that can ever happen to a person.

ACTOR: And there's all kinds of love. You can love your family.

ACTOR: Or your country.

ACTOR: Or your friends.

ACTOR: Or that special, certain someone.

ACTOR: The next letter is W.

ACTOR: No, it's not.

ACTOR: That's what the sign says.

ACTOR: It's upside down.

ACTOR: The next letter is M.

ACTOR: M is for Mom.

ACTOR: My mother met Monique in a unique New York boutique.

ACTOR: A boutique? I bet shopping there takes a lot of money.

ACTOR: Money starts with M.

ACTOR D: And so does marshmallows.

ACTOR P: Out!

ACTOR D: Mashed potatoes?

ACTOR P: You heard me, out!

ACTOR: Hey, do you hear that?

ACTOR: Yes. M is for music.

ACTOR: I love the way things fit together.
  The sun and wind that moves the weather,
  Flowers in bloom, mountain streams,
  Children's laughter, lovers' dreams, and
  It seems to me that it can be such a beautiful world
  If you have eyes to see.

  The oceans' roar, the quiet of space,
  The kind of peace that fills this place.
  A blessing rain that helps things grow,
  So much to learn, so much to know.
  It seems to me that it can be such a beautiful world
  If you have eyes to see.

  All life's a gift, one day at a time.
  It's up to us to find the reason and rhyme.
  It seems to me that it can be such a beautiful world
  If you have eyes, and you have eyes,
  Yes, you have eyes to see.

ACTOR: We sure do live in a beautiful place.

ACTOR: Yea, it's fun to go hiking and see all the mountains, birds, and plants.

ACTOR: Yep, nature sure is something.

ACTOR: And nature starts with N. That's the next letter.

ACTOR: But just what is nature?

ACTOR: Well, it can be hurricanes, and thunderstorms, and tidal waves, and floods.

ACTOR: That sounds scary.

ACTOR: But nature is also flowers, rainbows, plants, and oceans.

ACTOR: That sounds beautiful.

ACTOR: It is beautiful and that's why we should try to keep it that way.

ACTOR: By not littering.

ACTOR: And helping to clean up the beaches.

ACTOR: Planting trees.

ACTOR: Uh oh, here comes the food fairy.

ACTOR D: N is for noodles and nachos.

ACTOR Q: Yes, but it's also for *no*.

ACTOR R: Yes is for no?

ACTOR Q: Yes. I mean no. I mean it's important to learn when to say no.

ACTOR R: It is?

ACTOR Q: Yes.

ACTOR R: No.

ACTOR Q: Yes, it is.

ACTOR R: No, I was just practicing.

ACTOR Q: Oh.

ACTOR: You're right. O is the next letter.

ACTOR: O is a letter. And it's a word.

ACTOR: Oh?

ACTOR: Oh, yeah.

ACTOR: Uh, oh.

ACTOR: Oh, what?

ACTOR: Oh, no.

ACTOR: Oh, wow.

ACTOR: Oh …

ACTOR: What now?

ACTOR: I gotta P.

ACTOR: Now?

ACTOR: Yep. Here it is. *(Holds up card with letter P.)*

ACTOR: Ah, yes, the letter P is practically perfect for tongue twisting. As we all know, Peter Piper picked pilau papaya.

ACTOR: P is for puppets! *(Brings out puppets.)*

ACTOR D: *(A duet with puppet)* P is for peaches and peanut butter, pineapple pizza, popcorn and pretzels, pork and pickles, poke and poi, peas and pasta.

ACTOR: P also stands for pollution. Like broken bottles, and candy wrappers, and soda cans, and plastic straws.

ACTOR: I get the picture. So P stands for pollution, which is bad.

ACTOR: And peace, which would be wonderful.

ACTOR: What's peace?

ACTOR: That's when there's no fighting or wars and people just get along.

ACTOR: A long what? A long rope? A long time?

ACTOR: Quiet.

ACTOR: Who, me?

ACTOR: Quiet starts with Q and that's the next letter.

ACTOR S: Quick.

ACTOR: What's your hurry?

ACTOR S: No, quick starts with Q.

ACTOR: And so does queen, and here comes her royal highness now. *(QUEEN enters.)*

ACTOR T: What is your wish, your majesty?

QUEEN: Bring to me the royal hypnotist.

ACTOR T: Yes, your majesty.

QUEEN: I'd like something with the letter Q, please.

ACTOR T: Certainly. Right away. You are getting sleepy, sleepy. Your eyelids are getting heavy. *(Someone else snores.)* Not you. That's it, your majesty, now when I clap my hands, you'll think that you're a duck. *(Claps hands, QUEEN quacks.)* That's right, your majesty, quack starts with Q. *(To the audience)* Should I snap her out of it? Not yet? OK, well, let's give her a big hand. *(QUEEN exits quacking at the sound of the applause.)*

ACTOR: What letter follows Q, kids?

ACTOR: R. Right. Right as rain.

ACTOR: Round and round the rugged rock, the ragged rascal ran.

ACTOR: R is for rocket. Which can be good. Rockets have helped take us into space.

ACTOR: Yeah, rockets.

ACTOR: Which can be bad.

ACTOR: Huh?

ACTOR: Rockets can drop bombs on people.

ACTOR: A bomb? That would put a dent in my day.

ACTOR: Uh oh, here comes Miss Munchie ...

ACTOR D: R is for rice, raisins, rigatoni, ramen, ravioli, roast beef, and root beer floats. Yum.

ACTOR: What's the next letter?

ACTOR: I'll give you a hint. Sailing, swimming, and summertime.

ACTOR U: I got it! Ocean. You go sailing and swimming in the ocean. The letter is O.

ACTOR: We did O already.

ACTOR U: Oh.

ACTOR: The next letter is S.

ACTOR: She sells seashells by the seashore.

ACTOR D: She should have sold shrimp soup or spam spaghetti.

ACTOR: She should?

ACTOR D: Or shish kabob, sushi, or salami and salad sandwiches.

ACTOR: So you say.

ACTOR: S is for safety.

ACTOR V: Like always look both ways before brushing your teeth.

ACTOR: That's crossing the road.

ACTOR V: Whatever.

ACTOR: Safety tip number one! S is for stop, as in stop, drop, and roll. That's what you do if you're on fire.

ACTOR: I don't want to be on fire.

ACTOR: Safety tip number two — don't play with matches and never play with gasoline.

ACTOR: Safety tip number three — S is for strangers. Never talk to strangers.

ACTOR: Even if they're on fire.

ACTOR: Last safety tip! S is for seatbelt. Always wear your seatbelt when you're in a car.

ACTOR: The next letter is T.

ACTOR: T is for theatre. We're in a little theatre, and this play is a piece of theatre.

ACTOR: And one of the most famous scenes in the theatre is the balcony scene from *Romeo and Juliet*.

ACTOR O: Is it time?

ACTOR: Yes, finally. Go on.

ACTOR O: I can't. I can't do it. I can't remember my lines.

ACTOR: You'll do fine. Look. There she is.

ACTOR O: Wow. But soft, what light through yonder window breaks. It is the east, and Juliet is the sun.

ACTOR: Oh, Romeo. Oh, Romeo, a kiss for you, my Romeo. *(ACTOR O playing Romeo faints and is carried Off-stage.)*

ACTOR: What else can the letter T stand for?

ACTOR D: T stands for tea and Twinkies, tacos and tamales, tuna and tomatoes, tootsie rolls and toothpaste and for teeth which I use to tear into my taffy.

ACTOR: Your teeth are important, so remember to brush and floss and don't chew rocks.

ACTOR: And T is for tantrum. *(Cries.)*

ACTOR: Don't start that. Look! It's tongue twister time.

ACTOR: Ted told Tina's teacher she teased Tom ten times. Ted's a tattletale.

ACTOR W: Next letter, please. What's the next letter?

ACTOR X: U.

ACTOR W: I'm asking you.

ACTOR X: I'm telling you. It's U.

ACTOR W: It's me?

ACTOR X: No, U.

ACTOR W: I'm confused.

ACTOR X: As usual. U is for usual and unusual.

ACTOR D: I'm hungry.

ACTOR: As usual.

ACTOR D: But I can't think of what to eat.

ACTOR: For you, that's unusual.

ACTOR: U is for the whole universe, which is us in this room.

ACTOR: In this city.

ACTOR: In this state.

ACTOR: In the United States of America.

ACTOR: On this planet.

ACTOR: In this solar system.

ACTOR: In the Milky Way galaxy.

ACTOR D: Milky Way? Now that's a candy bar.

ACTOR: Out!

ACTOR D: OK, OK. I'm going. *(Exits.)*

ACTOR: We're almost to the end of the alphabet. What's the next letter?

ACTOR: V. V is for very, very, very something.

ACTOR: I know, vegetables. You've got to eat your vegetables.

ACTOR D: *(Enters.)* Did someone say eat?

ACTOR: Vegetables.

ACTOR D: Vegetables? Yum. Zucchini, carrots, broccoli, lettuce, not to forget squash, tomatoes, cucumbers, sprouts —

ACTOR: Next letter!

ACTOR: M?

ACTOR: Upside down again.

ACTOR: W?

ACTOR: Wendal wondered why the wishing well wouldn't work.

ACTOR: W-O-W, wow. What's next?

ACTOR Y: X is for … is for … well, it's real helpful for playing Tic Tac Toe.

ACTOR Z: Y.

ACTOR Y: Why what?

ACTOR Z: No, Y. It's the next letter.

ACTOR Y: I see.

ACTOR Z: Not the letter C. The letter is Y.

ACTOR Y: Oh.

ACTOR Z: Not O. The next to last letter in the alphabet is —

ACTOR Y: Y.

ACTOR Z: Yes, Y.

ACTOR Y: I don't know why.

ACTOR Z: Never mind.

ACTOR: Y is for you. And where would we be without you? And you. And you. *(Continues through the audience, pointing.)*

ACTOR: Yes, you have been a great audience for us. And we thank you for coming to see our show.

ACTOR: Hey, wait. Look.

(An actor is snoring at the side of the stage.)

ACTOR: I think he's trying to tell you something.

ACTOR: It looks like he's catching some Zs

ACTOR: Oh, Z, that's right. Z is the last letter of the alphabet.

ACTOR: Can you think of any words that start with Z?

ACTOR: Zero.

ACTOR: Then I guess we're done. It's time for our closing song, and if you know the words, you're welcome to sing along.

ACTOR: This is the song that never ends,

ACTOR: Yes, it goes on and on, my friends,

ACTOR: Some people started singing it not knowing what it was,

ACTOR: And they'll just keep on singing it forever just because ...

    (ALL exit through the audience singing.)

169. No Play

This is a play attempting to break many of the rules of performing and is inspired by Beckett's *Waiting For Godot* and theatre of the absurd.

MAX: *(Walks out On-stage, stares at the audience, then shouts into the wings, stage left.)* My friend, you may enter!

MEL: *(Enters from stage right.)* Thank you. Where shall we begin?

MAX: But we have begun.

MEL: The play, I mean. Which play shall we do for the people?

MAX: No play.

MEL: I beg your pardon?

MAX: No begging. No play.

MEL: But, my character —

MAX: No characters needed.

MEL: Well, then, a plot, perhaps?

MAX: No. Nothing.

MEL: You're being a bit negative.

MAX: Yes, I am.

MEL: No, you don't understand.

MAX: Yes, I do, and the answer is no play.

MEL: But I'm all dressed up. Tell you what, I'll go out and enter again.

MAX: Stop!

MEL: Who, me?

MAX: Is there anyone else on-stage to speak to?

MEL: You're not supposed to admit that we're on a stage.

MAX: My mind's made up. No play will take place on this very stage.

Mel: No dialogue?

MAX: Shhhh.

MEL: *(Pauses, thinks the situation over, then whispers.)* You can't have a play with no talking.

MAX: Exactly.

MEL: You spoke.

MAX: Did not.

MEL: Don't deny it.

MAX: I don't hear anything. Listen. *(Silence)*

MEL: No, you listen. We can't just make up the whole thing.

MAX: You're right.

MEL: There's no depth of character.

MAX: Well put.

MEL: But what do I want?

MAX: Nothing.

MEL: Nothing?

MAX: No thing. No play.

MEL: No plot? No conflict?

MAX: No motivation.

MEL: No direction?

MAX: Like I say, no play.

MEL: Alright, if that's the way you want it, we can just stand here.

MAX: Fine. *(Long pause)*

MEL: You can't just stand there.

MAX: I am standing here.

MEL: Well, no one's going to watch you just standing there.

MAX: They're watching. *(Points to audience.)*

MEL: And waiting.

MAX: For what? Godot?

MEL: For a play. You know, to play, to perform. That supreme moment of artistic ecstasy. *(Pause)* My big line.

MAX: Just say it then.

MEL: Now?

MAX: You might as well. You're already talking.

MEL: But we've got to build up to it.

MAX: How?

MEL: You know — action, theme, subtext, gestures, blocking, props, lighting, facial expressions. It's got to mean something, doesn't it?

MAX: What can I say? We are actors in no play, symbolic of some writer's frustration.

MEL: No play?

MAX: Victims of unclear conflicts, discarded stage tricks, ideas that fail to come.

MEL: But my big line?

MAX: Say it and let there be peace.

MEL: How is this all going to end? *(Blackout. Or MAX and MEL bow their heads and freeze in position until, or if, the audience applauds.)*

170. Who Stay Rockin'?

Setting: The Office of Perfect Paradise Promoters

ACTOR 1: Where's that guy with the permits?

ACTOR 2: Shhhh. I'm on the phone. *(Into phone)* Great. That's the best news I've heard all day. I'll e-mail you the contracts. Talk to you soon. Good-bye.

ACTOR 1: What good news?

ACTOR 2: That was Pete Townsend's manager. We got 'em! We're going to have The Who for our third act in the Big Bands Reunion Concert.

ACTOR 1: The Who? That's fantastic. And with the group Yes already lined up …

ACTOR 2: And don't forget … *(Cues CD and sings)* American woman, stay away from me …

ACTOR 1 and 2: The Guess Who!

(There's a knock at the door. POLICE OFFICER enters.)

POLICE OFFICER: Excuse me. Is this the Office for Perfect Paradise Promoters?

ACTOR 2: Yes, it is. Are you the guy the police commissioner was sending over with those permits we need for our concert?

POLICE OFFICER: Yes, sir. Let's see, I got parking permits, port-a-potty permits, and police protection permits.

ACTOR 1: Great. Where do we sign?

POLICE OFFICER: Well, first, I gotta fill in the names of the performing acts.

ACTOR 2: Sure. Right. It's gonna be a triple bill.

POLICE OFFICER: Bill who?

ACTOR 1: No, he means there's gonna be three bands.

POLICE OFFICER: Oh, I see … and who will be playing?

ACTOR 2: Yes, we just found out.

ACTOR 1: It's gonna be the next best thing to a Beatles reunion.

POLICE OFFICER: Who is?

ACTOR 2: I'd say so.

ACTOR 1: And of course, there's The Guess Who.

POLICE OFFICER: The who?

ACTOR 1: That's right, and The Guess Who.

POLICE OFFICER: I'm not sure, but you said there's gonna be three bands.

ACTOR 2: That's right. We forgot, Yes.

POLICE OFFICER: Yes?

ACTOR 1: That's right. That's all three of them.

POLICE OFFICER: I've got to write down their names.

ACTOR 2: You haven't done it yet?

POLICE OFFICER: I would, if you just tell me who's gonna be playing.

ACTOR 1: And The Guess Who.

POLICE OFFICER: Yes?

ACTOR 2: There you go. That's all of them.

POLICE OFFICER: Let me get this straight ... these are rock and roll bands ...

ACTOR 1: The best.

POLICE OFFICER: And who will be playing first?

ACTOR 2: Well, maybe Yes.

ACTOR 1: We haven't decided.

POLICE OFFICER: Well, who's gonna play last?

ACTOR 2: The Guess Who.

POLICE OFFICER: I have no idea, but I'd like to get these permits filled out.

ACTOR 1: So would we.

POLICE OFFICER: So just tell me slowly and clearly the names of the three bands.

ACTOR 2: We said Yes and The Who.

POLICE OFFICER: Just one more time so I'm sure I got it right, OK?

ACTOR 1: If you insist.

POLICE OFFICER: Yes, please. Now, rock group number one ...

ACTOR 2: Yes.

POLICE OFFICER: Yes?

ACTOR 1: Then The Who.

POLICE OFFICER: Who?

ACTOR 2: That's right. You're doin' great. Then finally, The Guess Who.

POLICE OFFICER: You want me to guess?

ACTOR 1: We want the permits!

POLICE OFFICER: Then who's playing?

ACTOR 1: Don't you like rock and roll?

POLICE OFFICER: Yes!

ACTOR 2: That's one group.

POLICE OFFICER: Who?

ACTOR 1: That's the second.

POLICE OFFICER: What's the third group?

ACTOR 2: The Guess Who!

POLICE OFFICER: I give up. Here, you fill in the names. *(Exits. Fade to black.)*

171. Love at First Sight

Setting: A coffee shop

(CALI is seated, sipping coffee, and reading a braille book. JAMES enters, crosses to her table, and gestures for permission to sit. CALI appears to be ignoring him, so he speaks.)

JAMES: Excuse me …

CALI: Yes?

JAMES: Do you mind if I sit here?

CALI: Well …

JAMES: Since there aren't any other seats available …

CALI: Alright.

JAMES: *(Extending his hand)* My name's James.

CALI: *(Doesn't shake his hand.)* Mine's Cali.

JAMES: Cali?

CALI: It's short for California, where I was born. My mom's got this thing for weird names.

JAMES: You're from California?

CALI: Nevada, actually. It's kind of confusing, but you see, my mom was on a train passing through California, on her way to be with my grandmother in Oregon because she was about to give birth to me … am I confusing you?

JAMES: I'm fascinated.

CALI: So anyway, something about the motion of the train got Mom's contractions started and the next thing she knows, here I come, two months early, delivered by a lady ticket collector.

JAMES: Wow, that must have been something to see.

CALI: I wouldn't know.

JAMES: Well, you were too young.

CALI: And I can't see.

JAMES: I beg your pardon?

CALI: I can't see, James. I'm blind.

JAMES: I'm sorry.

CALI: It's not your fault.

JAMES: So that's why you were leaving me standing there. I thought you were either snobby or just rude.

CALI: Now I'm the one who's sorry.

JAMES: Let's just call it even.

CALI: Deal.

JAMES: So how … I mean … why …

CALI: Why am I blind?

JAMES: If you don't mind my asking …

CALI: Not at all. It was complications from being a premature baby. The wrong mix of oxygen in the incubator can cause blindness.

JAMES: I see...

CALI: Well, not me. Not that I can remember.

JAMES: Oh, that's awful.

CALI: Is it? Why?

JAMES: Well, I ... I don't know ...

CALI: You see, I have nothing to compare it to. I don't feel like I'm missing anything.

JAMES: Wow ... it's hard to imagine.

CALI: What is?

JAMES: Not being able to see. What's that like. I mean, are you in the dark?

CALI: What's dark? I'm here with you.

JAMES: You don't see anything? *(Waves his hand in front of her face.)*

CALI: No. But I can feel your hand near my face.

JAMES: No shadows? No bright lights?

CALI: Just what is light, anyway?

JAMES: Light?

CALI: I hear people talk about it all the time. "I have seen the light!" Or "You light up my life." But I just don't get it.

JAMES: It's hard to explain.

CALI: Tell me.

JAMES: Light, huh. Well ... it ... it shines.

CALI: Shines?

JAMES: Yeah, like in a beam of light.

CALI: I've felt a balance beam at gymnastics.

JAMES: It's not that kind of beam. It's not something you feel.

CALI: But I have felt it. I've felt the sunlight on my face, the warmth of a fire. Here, feel my hand. It's warm, isn't it?

JAMES: Yes ...

CALI: But does it glow? Does it give off light, like the sun?

JAMES: Well ...

CALI: Or a fire?

JAMES: Your hand reflects the light.

CALI: Reflects?

JAMES: Like a mirror.

CALI: Which feels like glass to me. Through the looking glass.

JAMES: A mirror has a reflective coating on the back of the glass.

CALI: I've heard that *to reflect* means to think about something. Maybe you only think you see me.

JAMES: You're playing with me.

CALI: Playing with words. That's what I do. I'm a writer.
JAMES: I'm impressed.
CALI: You jest.
JAMES: I guess.
CALI: Oh, yes ...
JAMES: And are you working on something now? Poetry or a book?
CALI: I'm always working. Right now it's a short story. I want to call it *The Rainbow's End.*
JAMES: I like it already. Is it finished?
CALI: It needs some work. I could use your help, actually.
JAMES: Sure. But how?
CALI: Can you tell me about rainbows. I've never seen one.
JAMES: Rainbows? That's not easy to explain.
CALI: Who said things have got to be easy?
JAMES: OK. OK. Well, a rainbow is something that happens when there's sun and rain at the same time.
CALI: Oh, I'm familiar with rain. There's the kind that soaks you 'til you shiver. Or a light mist that you can just barely feel against your face and eyelashes.
JAMES: Good. So imagine there's a misty rain over the mountains.
CALI: Mountains?
JAMES: Don't play with me. This is hard enough.
CALI: Keep going.
JAMES: OK. So it's raining, and when the sun hits those raindrops, it splits into all the colors.
CALI: And what are colors?
JAMES: That's ... that's a good question. Colors. I guess you could compare it to textures in fabric — some colors are silky and smooth, and some are rough, like denim in a pair of jeans.
CALI: Can you touch a rainbow?
JAMES: No. If you chase it, it runs away.
CALI: Like a dream.
JAMES: Yeah, like a dream. *(A pause)*
CALI: Can I touch your face?
JAMES: Why?
CALI: So I can *see* you.
JAMES: Sure. I'd like that.
CALI: *(She gently runs her hands over his features.)* Are you smiling?
JAMES: I can't help it.
CALI: *(Puts his hand to her face.)* Now you tell me. What do I look like?
JAMES: You look good ... I mean ... you're good looking.
CALI: I don't understand *looks.*

JAMES: Well, you're easy on my eyes ... um ... that doesn't explain anything, does it?

CALI: Keep trying.

JAMES: Honestly? You're beautiful ... warm, like the sun on your face. Like the sound of kids playing.

CALI: I'm beginning to see.

JAMES: You're the kind of girl a guy would be proud to be seen with, I mean, be with.

CALI: *(Holding up her hand to touch his face)* James, can I see you again?

172. Thesaurus Murder Mystery

Cast:

Anthony Livingston — son of Dr. Livingston

Ashley Livingston — black sheep son of Dr. Livingston

Allissa Livingston — spoiled daughter of Dr. Livingston

Lani Livingston — Ashley's wife

Cop

Grandma

(At rise, the actors are frozen in a scene while COP gives the brief introduction.)

COP: My name's Friday. I'm a cop. The police. An officer of the law. I've seen some strange cases, but this one was a doozy. A synonym saga so soaked in secrets and subversion, well, you'll see. It started like this ...

(COP steps into the scene with the other actors.)

ANTHONY: Oh, thank you for coming so quickly, officer.

ASHLEY: We appreciate it.

ALLISSA: We're grateful.

COP: Yes, now what is this about a murder, the homicide you phoned in?

(ALL step aside to reveal the body.)

LANI: It's Doctor Livingston.

ANTHONY: He's been stabbed!

COP: He's dead?

ASHLEY: Deceased.

ALLISSA: Bought the farm.

LANI: Bit the bullet.

GRANDMA: Rung down life's curtain and joined the choir eternal.

ANTHONY: Yes, Grandma.

GRANDMA: His flame has gone out.

ASHLEY: Yes, Grandma.

GRANDMA: He is no more.

ALLISSA: Grandma!

GRANDMA: Well, he's Saint Peter's problem now.

COP: And just when did this happen? What time?

LANI: We heard a scream around nine o'clock, rushed in here to his study, and found him dead on the floor.

GRANDMA: A goner.

ASHLEY: Kaput. Mort. Stiff.

COP: So we can assume this bloody crime occurred right here.

ALLISSA: In the house.

ASHLEY: The Livingston domicile.

GRANDMA: Home sweet home.

COP: Now we need a motive; a reason for the stabbing. Who had it in for him? Did he have any enemies?

(ALL shake their heads "no.")

COP: People who wanted him dead?

(ALL look guilty.)

GRANDMA: He hardly went out. Just us family here.

COP: Then why would someone kill him?

GRANDMA: Could be the money.

ANTHONY: The inheritance.

ASHLEY: The fortune.

LANI: The whole enchilada.

COP: He was rich?

ALLISSA: Well to do.

LANI: Quite comfortable

ASHLEY: Rolling in it.

COP: Ah ha! And did he have a companion? A friend, perhaps a woman? A mistress? A lover?

ALLISSA: Nah, he was too old.

GRANDMA: That's what you think.

ASHLEY: He was in his latter days.

LANI: Kinda wrinkled.

ANTHONY: An antique.

COP: Who's his next of kin? Closest relative? The person who gets the money.

ASHLEY: Just us brothers and sisters.

GRANDMA: Any one of them could have done it.

ANTHONY: Grandma!

ALLISSA: Or someone with an accomplice. *(Indicating LANI and ASHLEY)*

GRANDMA: Perhaps a conspiracy between the lot of them.

ANTHONY: Grandma!

COP: Were there any clues? Evidence? Telltale signs? Fingerprints? Spatter pattern? DNA?

ASHLEY: Not a bit. But I'll tell you what I think. I think she did it! *(Points to ALLISSA.)*

ALLISSA: I never. I'm innocent. Faultless. That's a totally capricious accusation. I'm pure as the driven snow.

ASHLEY: Yea, right.

COP: Well, can any of you prove you didn't do it?

ANTHONY: You mean an alibi?

ALLISSA: We were all in the library at the same time.

ASHLEY: Except for bathroom breaks.

GRANDMA: I have a condition.

LANI: I had to powder my nose.

ANTHONY: I made a few phone calls.

COP: Enough! I've figured it out! It was you. *(Points to LANI.)*

ASHLEY: That temptress.

ALLISSA: Gold digger.

GRANDMA: Slut.

ALL: Grandma!

LANI: Alright! I confess. I did it. But it was an accident. *(To herself)* Yeah, that's the ticket. *(To the group)* An accident, I tell ya. He was showing me his antique knife and he tripped and fell on it.

ALLISSA: She's lying.

GRANDMA: Fibbin'.

ASHLEY: She's playin' you.

ANTHONY: Don't believe her.

COP: Oh, I can tell when a murderer's lyin'.

ALLISSA: How?

COP: Their lips move.

LANI: OK, copper. You got me. I'm guilty. I stabbed the old goat.

ALLISSA: But why'd ya kill him?

LANI: He wanted to … you know. But he disgusted me. I was repulsed by him. Why he wanted to …

GRANDMA: I've heard enough. She confessed. It's the hoosegow for you, hussy.

COP: You're gonna see some serious jail time.

ANTHONY: Goin' to Disneyland.

ALLISSA: The big house.

ASHLEY: You're getting a cell and we don't mean phone.

ALLISSA: Arrest her.

ANTHONY: Cuff her.

GRANDMA: Book her.

173. Fish Shop

A scene for two students inspired by Monty Python's *Dead Parrot* sketch.

ACTOR 1: Excuse me, I was just passing by and thought to myself, "Perhaps I should stop in this quaint little shop and purchase some delights from the deep."

ACTOR 2: Say what?

ACTOR 1: I want to buy some fish.

ACTOR 2: K-den. Now you talkin'. This one fish shop, you know.

ACTOR 1: Just give me a moment to look over the selections. Ah, yes. I believe I'll have some Mahi-mahi.

ACTOR 2: Sorry, no can. Da boat no catch any.

ACTOR 1: I see, then I'll settle for Ono.

ACTOR 2: *(Mimes looking in the freezer.)* Oh, no ...

ACTOR 1: Yes, Ono will be fine.

ACTOR 2: What I meant was, "Oh, no, the cat wen' eat um."

ACTOR 1: Then how about Mackerel?

ACTOR 2: Sold outta Mackerel. Good bait, dat one.

ACTOR 1: How about Papio?

ACTOR 2: Yesterday, yes. Today, sold out.

ACTOR 1: Codfish?

ACTOR 2: Sorry.

ACTOR 1: Tilapia?

ACTOR 2: Not today.

ACTOR 1: Salmon?

ACTOR 2: Outta season.

ACTOR 1: Sardines.

ACTOR 2: No can. Da shipment's late.

ACTOR 1: Swordfish?

ACTOR 2: Last week, had —

ACTOR 1: Do you have any Octopus.

ACTOR 2: Tako?

ACTOR 1: Squid.

ACTOR 2: Oh, yeah, we got squid.

ACTOR 1: Finally. I'll take a whole half pound.

ACTOR 2: *(Checks the freezer.)* Wait a minute ...

ACTOR 1: What's the matter?

ACTOR 2: Da buggah looks kind a runny. Even da cat wouldn' eat um.

ACTOR 1: How about Halibut.

ACTOR 2: Just sold the last one.

ACTOR 1: Sturgeon?

ACTOR 2: Nope.
ACTOR 1: Flounder?
ACTOR 2: Uh, no.
ACTOR 1: Perch?
ACTOR 2: Sorry.
ACTOR 1: Trout?
ACTOR 2: All out.
ACTOR 1: Butterfish?
ACTOR 2: Fresh or frozen?
ACTOR 1: Fresh.
ACTOR 2: All out.
ACTOR 1: Frozen!
ACTOR 2: That too.
ACTOR 1: Then I guess I'll just have to settle for tuna fish.
ACTOR 2: Sorry, we no carry dat one.
ACTOR 1: You don't carry tuna fish? Tuna happens to be the most popular fish in the entire world!
ACTOR 2: Not around here.
ACTOR 1: And just what is the most popular fish in these parts?
ACTOR 2: Opakapaka. Red Snapper.
ACTOR 1: And do you, indeed, have any? I ask, expecting the answer, "no."
ACTOR 2: No, sorry.
ACTOR 1: Do you, in fact, have any fish at all in the entire store?
ACTOR 2: No. I was just pulling your leg.
ACTOR 1: I've had enough! I'm leaving! *(Starts to exit.)*
ACTOR 2: Try wait, try wait. I do know where you can get some fish.
ACTOR 1: Well, that's better. Where?
ACTOR 2: In da ocean, bra. Laters. *(Exits.)*

174. The English Teacher Gets a Language Lesson

STUDENT 2: Yo, teach.
STUDENT 1: Wurd up, dog.
TEACHER: Say what?
STUDENT 2: What's the haps?
TEACHER: Are you two speaking English?
STUDENT 1: Like, dir. Get with it.
STUDENT 2: Catch up with the times, teach.
TEACHER: I suppose you're right. After all, language is always changing.
STUDENT 1: How can you tell?
TEACHER: I've been around longer than you two. And I know a thing or two.

STUDENT 2: Whachu talkin' 'bout, homey?

TEACHER: Well, homey ... take for example *shell shock.*

STUDENT 1: What's that?

TEACHER: That's a term that goes way back to World War One. It's meant to describe the stress a soldier feels from coming up against intense combat.

STUDENT 2: You mean he wigs out?

TEACHER: If that means it can drive a person crazy, yes.

STUDENT 1: The guy goes nutso?

TEACHER: It can happen. When World War Two came along, they started to call it *battle fatigue.*

STUDENT 2: Fatigue? You mean like he's tired of war?

TEACHER: In so many words. Then in the Vietnam War they called it *post-traumatic stress disorder.*

STUDENT 1: So it keeps changing.

STUDENT 2: New war, new words.

TEACHER: That's the way it is with language. Another example would be *toilet paper.* I believe they call it *bathroom tissue* now.

STUDENT 1: Right. What else?

TEACHER: Well, there's sneakers ...

STUDENT 2: What's that?

TEACHER: I believe they call them running shoes now.

STUDENT 1: I get it. No more sneaking around. It's all run, baby, run.

TEACHER: And then there's *the dump.*

STUDENT 2: Is that what I think it is?

TEACHER: Now they call it the *landfill.* And how about *used cars.*

STUDENT 1: What about them?

TEACHER: Now they're starting to call them *previously owned transportation.*

STUDENT 2: Because it sounds better?

TEACHER: Right. And when I was a kid, if I got sick, I had to go see the doctor.

STUDENT 1: Now it's an HMO.

STUDENT 2: Homo?

TEACHER: It stands for Health Maintenance Organization, or Wellness Center.

STUDENT 1: Sounds like we've got to learn more words for everything.

TEACHER: That's right. Welcome to my world ... and yours.

STUDENT 2: This is cool. Are there any others?

TEACHER: Lots. In my day, the poor folks lived in *slums.*

STUDENT 1: And now?

TEACHER: It's call *substandard housing in the inner city.*

STUDENT 2: Why do the words change?

TEACHER: I guess to make things sound better. You're not a *garbage man*, you're a *sanitation engineer*. You're not *deaf*, you're *hearing impaired*. We soften the language for the things we fear, like getting old.

STUDENT 2: Like you?

TEACHER: Easy. People don't get *old* anymore.

STUDENT 1: They don't?

TEACHER: They become *senior citizens*.

STUDENT 2: So we find better words for things we're afraid of?

TEACHER: Exactly. Like death. We don't want to die, just *pass away*.

STUDENT 1: Meet our maker.

TEACHER: Or *expire*, like a driver's license.

STUDENT 2: Like my Grandma. Mom says she's *singing with the angels* now.

STUDENT 1: Wow, teach, when it comes to language, you be bad.

TEACHER: And that's good?

STUDENT 2: Wurd up.

175. Vaudeville or What People Did for Fun before They Invented TV

The lines in this collection of jokes appear as STUDENT accompanied by a number so the director can assign them to any student or teacher who fits the part.

STUDENT 1: Howzit, everybody! For our show today, we want to take you back.

STUDENT 2: Way back. Way, way, way, waaaay back.

STUDENT 3: Back to the days before you were born. Before there was television. Before there was even movies.

STUDENT 4: Dinosaurs?

STUDENT 5: Not that far back. Around the time of the Wild Wild West.

STUDENT 6: We want to show you what Vaudeville was like.

STUDENT 7: Where people would perform live on a stage or in a saloon, telling jokes.

STUDENT 8: No kidding?

STUDENT 9: I'm not joking.

STUDENT 10: You said there were going to be jokes.

STUDENT 11: Then we better get started.

STUDENT 12: Well, women are funny. Take my girlfriend. Please.

STUDENT 13: Hey, what did the cannibal say when he ate the clown?

STUDENT 14: I don't know. What?

STUDENT 15: Does this taste funny to you?

STUDENT 16: You think you're so smart.

STUDENT 17: I am, ask me a question. Any question.

STUDENT 18: OK, what two days of the week start with the letter T?

STUDENT 17: That's easy: today and tomorrow.

STUDENT 19: OK, here's a harder one. How many seconds are there in a year?

STUDENT 17: That's not hard. There's twelve.

STUDENT 20: Twelve?

STUDENT 17: Sure. January second. February second. March second …

STUDENT 21: Did you hear about the nose that went to volleyball tryouts?

STUDENT 22: The nose?

STUDENT 23: He kept yelling, "Pick me, pick me!"

STUDENT 24: I'm kind of worried. My doctor says I've only got ten left.

STUDENT 25: Ten what? Ten years? Ten months?

STUDENT 24: I don't know. He just said ten, nine, eight, seven …

STUDENT 26: You got to be careful about catching diseases from birds.

STUDENT 27: You mean bird flu?

STUDENT 26: No, it's something you get from kissing them. It's called Chirpes. I hear it's untweetable.

STUDENT 28: Speaking of birds, do you know why seagulls live near the sea?

STUDENT 29: Why?

STUDENT 28: Because if they lived by the bay, they'd be bagels.

STUDENT 30: I had to go to my doctor the other day because both my ears were red and swollen.

STUDENT 31: How did your ears get like that?

STUDENT 30: I was ironing my clothes, the phone rang, and I picked up the iron by mistake.

STUDENT 32: What about your other ear?

STUDENT 30: The jerk called back.

STUDENT 33: I'm not eating Mexican food ever again.

STUDENT 34: Why not?

STUDENT 33: I just found out that *taco* spelled backwards is *o, cat.*

STUDENT 35: My teacher is so dumb. The other day he called the police to report that someone stole the steering wheel out of his car.

STUDENT 36: How awful.

STUDENT 35: Not really, the cops showed up and found him sitting in the backseat.

STUDENT 37: Well, I asked my teacher if she would punish me for something I didn't do, and she said, "Of course not." So I said, "Great, 'cause I didn't do my homework."
STUDENT 38: Well, we're out of time.
STUDENT 39: We've got plenty of time.
STUDENT 40: We're out of jokes.
STUDENT 41: Gotta run. Hope you all had fun.

176. Hello, I'm Leaving

This scene is a dialogue to practice subtext. It is vague and ambiguous, allowing the actors to convey the subtext or meaning behind the lines by the way they say them, as well as their gestures and facial expressions. They can be friendly or fighting, joking or sad, etc.

STUDENT 1: Hi.
STUDENT 2: Hello.
STUDENT 1: Are you alright?
STUDENT 2: I think so.
STUDENT 1: Are you sure?
STUDENT 2: A little pain, here. That's all.
STUDENT 1: Anything I can do?
STUDENT 2: You've done quite enough.
STUDENT 1: I think we need to talk.
STUDENT 2: About what?
STUDENT 1: You know.
STUDENT 2: I'm leaving.
STUDENT 1: I knew it all along.

177. Whacky Commercials for Scene Practice

Hair So Cool

I look good. I know I look good. And you can look this good too with *Hair So Cool*. It comes in spray, gel, or handy stick roll-on. Come on. Isn't it time you started looking this good?

Air Arnolds

You snooze, you lose, but not in these shoes. Guaranteed to give you more bounce to the ounce. Air Arnolds. They're here to fire you up. So what are you waiting for? Get hopping.

As Your Stomach Turns

Will Jeff return from the dead to marry his ex-wife's sister? What will Dora say to her boyfriends Bill and Bob when they find out she's been dating the mailman? Will Connie ever come out of her coma to name Nathan's killer? Find out in this week's episode of *As Your Stomach Turns.* They put the soap in soap opera.

Moneymobile

Are you tired of driving the same old car? Do you want something that says style? Something that says, "bam," "pow," or "oooo la la"? Come drive a Moneymobile. It costs big bucks, but hey, aren't you worth it?

Kool Kine Cola

Hey, America, are you ready for a soft drink with zing? Step into a Kool Kine Cola and find out what a real refreshment can be. More vitamins than a truckload full of monkeys.

But hey, who's counting? The zing in this thing will rock your world.

Spring Pooper Scooper Super Sale

Pet World at Manure Marketplace announces it's Spring Pooper Scooper Super Sale. Hurry on down today and check out the latest in whale wallets, termite toothpicks, and pajamas for polar bears. Your pets will look their best and the first four hundred people through the door will receive free doggie deodorant.

Junk Food

ACTOR 1: Yuck. This food tastes like *junk.*

ACTOR 2: Well, it should. It's *Junk Food.*

ACTOR 2: But it tastes awful.

ACTOR 1: Yes, and it comes in six disgusting flavors.

ACTOR 2: No one would want to eat this.

ACTOR 1: Exactly. That's why it's the perfect way to lose weight. It's guaranteed to help prevent obsessive eating habits.

ACTOR 2: Cool. What's for dessert?

ACTOR 1: Liver-flavored ice cream with sawdust sprinkles. Remember, if it isn't *Junk Food,* you are eating too much.

Skunk

It's way cool. It's punk. It's *Skunk,* the most powerful cologne a man can wear. Just try it once and you'll agree you've never smelled anything like it. It comes in three sizes: handy pocket size, spray can, and money-saving five gallon bucket. You'll turn heads when you walk into a room wearing the scent of *Skunk.* Available only at Lungs Drug Stores.

Dr. Duke's Elixir of Life

Friends, and you are my friends, you've seen it advertised on TV, so it must be true, that Doctor Duke's amazing *Elixir of Life* is modern medicine's miracle answer to all your aches, ailments, and illnesses.

Yes, friends, whether you suffer from backache, heartache, or halitosis, Doctor Duke will clear it up while it clears you out.

Safe enough for a baby baboon's bathwater, it's a cure-all to beat all. It don't matter whether you're blind, bald, or brain dead, Doctor Duke will ease your wheezin', sneezin', bedwettin', warts, gas pains, or pimples.

Buy it by the case and say good-bye to the mumps, measles, and malaria. And folks, I am living proof that Doctor Duke does work cuz I can tell you I have been drinking this stuff all day and I swear I am feeling no pain. Thank you.

Chapter Nine
Careers in Drama and Getting Started in the Profession

I've included at the end of this section a listing of several of the jobs related to drama, movie making in particular, but such a list could be easily generated by the students themselves by going over the credits at the end of one of their favorite movies, pausing to discuss the various skills required for each job category.

Acting is a very competitive occupation with many people vying for a limited number of roles. I advise students intent on pursuing a career in acting to have a backup line of work to support themselves until that big break comes along. I warn them that they must be prepared to deal with disappointment and rejection. They must also not be discouraged about getting a small part since all roles in a production are important to the overall piece and offer a chance to shine.

Obviously, there is more work to be found for actors in big cities, with Los Angeles being a focal point for movie acting and New York City the mecca for stage work. Locally, there are some opportunities for paid acting work with local TV productions, commercials, and most community theatre roles offer experience but no pay, except for the occasional small stipends to cover transportation costs to and from rehearsals.

I strongly encourage students with a sincere desire to develop their talents to audition for community theatre productions if roles for younger actors are available. They should consider having a memorized monologue that shows their talents, a dance routine, and a song they enjoy singing. It helps to bring along sheet music for the song and know what key fits the student's range. They should also check out a copy of the script from the theatre hosting the production or find one online or through the library. They should read the entire play, see if any roles interest them, and then familiarize themselves with the scenes and dialogue involving the character(s) they're interested in trying out for. If they have past acting experience, it might be helpful to bring to the audition a brief resume and a photo of themselves.

Students should be encouraged to create their own opportunities. They can create talent shows for their school and friends, write their own scenes on topics that interest them, and recreate scenes from their favorite movies or plays. They can organize improv parties or improve their acting skills by memorizing monologues and scenes, taking voice lessons, dance classes, acting workshops, and keeping physically fit. The body is one of the actor's tools and needs to be kept in good working condition to meet the requirements of any role. They should practice their skills of observation, paying attention to people's ways of speaking, their mannerisms, posture, movement, and gestures. Observing people in everyday life can provide wonderful character studies and it's free. It's OK to try to mimic someone, preferably if that person is not present.

Finally, I suggest that the students read and research about acting, favorite actors, plays, and movies. It may be tough to make a living at acting, but if one simply wants to act, then money is not an issue. They can take classes, go to auditions, volunteer backstage, and videotape their own creations.

Drama Careers

Actor or actress
Set designer
Prop builder
Director
Camera operator
Makeup person
Casting director
Special effects artist
Choreographer
Grip — moves equipment
Lighting crew
Costume designer
Stunt person
Producers
Sound designer
Locations manager
Publicist

Glossary of Drama Terms

Ad lib: Making up a line of dialogue if you forget yours.

Audience: The people watching a performance.

Audition: Reading lines, singing, or dancing for the director of a play, movie, or commercial in hopes of getting a part.

Backstage: The area behind the stage that cannot be seen by the audience.

Blocking: Where and how an actor moves about the stage.

Character: The person an actor portrays — pretends to be — in a scene, play, TV show, or movie.

Cheating out: Standing on the stage in such a way that most of the audience can see the actor's face.

Costume: Clothes worn by an actor in a scene or play.

Covering: Making up dialogue if you or your fellow actors forget their lines.

Crossing: Moving from one area of the stage to another.

Cue: The signal to begin a spoken line or action, usually the line before your line or lines.

Curtain call: When the actors come out at the end of a performance to bow and accept the applause of the audience.

Dialogue: Spoken lines between two actors.

Exposition: The information given through dialogue during a scene that gives background information necessary to understanding the play.

Extemporaneous speaking: A speech that is made up on the spot by the speaker, not prepared in advance.

Gesture: A movement, usually with the hands and arms, expressing or supporting an idea or emotion.

The house: The area where the audience sits in a theatre.

Improvisation: Also known as improv, is a scene performed by actors who make up the lines of dialogue as they go along.

Monologue: Solo speech by an actor.

Pantomime: Also known as mime, is a scene with no talking or dialogue, often involving large gestures to *show* objects and communicate information.

Props: Small items or objects used by an actor in a scene.

Run-through: Practicing a play or scene from beginning to end.

Set: The space in which a play or scene takes place. The set can give context to when and where the play is happening.

Stage: The performance area in a theatre or auditorium.

Upstaging: Trying to steal a scene or take the focus away from others during a scene. It is not a polite thing to do.

Walk on: A small part in a play, usually with no lines.

Wings: The sides of the stage where actors can wait without being seen by the audience.

About the Author

Rod Martin has been a drama educator for over 30 years having worked in schools, community centers, and even a womens' prison. He is a published poet and playwright and a professional songwriter. Check out rodmartinmusic.com. He enjoys hiking, kayaking the coastlines of Hawaii, and planting a variety of trees and flowers at his rain forest country estate. He's accessible, too. You can call him to discuss the games at 808-239-2119 or you can email him at rodmartin@hawaii.rr.com.

Order Form

Meriwether Publishing Ltd.
PO Box 7710
Colorado Springs, CO 80933-7710
Phone: 800-937-5297   Fax: 719-594-9916
Website: www.meriwether.com

Please send me the following books:

_____	**Drama Games and Acting Exercises** **#BK-B311** by Rod Martin *177 games and activities*	**$17.95**
_____	**Acting Games for Individual Performers** **#BK-B297** by Gavin Levy *A comprehensive workbook of 110 acting exercises*	**$17.95**
_____	**Theatre Games for Young Peformers** **#BK-B188** by Maria C. Novelly *Improvisations and exercises for developing acting skills*	**$17.95**
_____	**Drama Games and Improvs #BK-B296** by Justine Jones and Mary Ann Kelley *Games for the classroom and beyond*	**$22.95**
_____	**Thirty Short Comedy Plays for Teens** **#BK-B292** by Laurie Allen *Plays for a variety of cast sizes*	**$16.95**
_____	**Improv Ideas #BK-B283** by Justine Jones and Mary Ann Kelley *A book of games and lists*	**$22.95**
_____	**112 Acting Games #BK-B277** by Gavin Levy *A comprehensive workbook of theatre games*	**$17.95**

These and other fine Meriwether Publishing books are available at your local bookstore or direct from the publisher. Prices subject to change without notice. Check our website or call for current prices.

Name: _____ email:_____

Organization name: _____

Address: _____

City: _____ State: _____

Zip: _____ Phone: _____

❑ **Check enclosed**

❑ **Visa / MasterCard / Discover / Am. Express #** _____

Signature: _____ *Expiration date:* _____ / _____
(required for credit card orders)

Colorado residents: Please add 3% sales tax.
Shipping: Include $3.95 for the first book and 75¢ for each additional book ordered.

❑ *Please send me a copy of your complete catalog of books and plays.*

Order Form

Meriwether Publishing Ltd.
PO Box 7710
Colorado Springs, CO 80933-7710
Phone: 800-937-5297 Fax: 719-594-9916
Website: www.meriwether.com

Please send me the following books:

_____ **Drama Games and Acting Exercises**   **$17.95**
#BK-B311
by Rod Martin
177 games and activities

_____ **Acting Games for Individual Performers**   **$17.95**
#BK-B297
by Gavin Levy
A comprehensive workbook of 110 acting exercises

_____ **Theatre Games for Young Peformers**   **$17.95**
#BK-B188
by Maria C. Novelly
Improvisations and exercises for developing acting skills

_____ **Drama Games and Improvs #BK-B296**   **$22.95**
by Justine Jones and Mary Ann Kelley
Games for the classroom and beyond

_____ **Thirty Short Comedy Plays for Teens**   **$16.95**
#BK-B292
by Laurie Allen
Plays for a variety of cast sizes

_____ **Improv Ideas #BK-B283**   **$22.95**
by Justine Jones and Mary Ann Kelley
A book of games and lists

_____ **112 Acting Games #BK-B277**   **$17.95**
by Gavin Levy
A comprehensive workbook of theatre games

These and other fine Meriwether Publishing books are available at your local bookstore or direct from the publisher. Prices subject to change without notice. Check our website or call for current prices.

Name: _____ email:_____

Organization name: _____

Address: _____

City: _____ State: _____

Zip: _____ Phone: _____

❑ **Check enclosed**

❑ **Visa / MasterCard / Discover / Am. Express #** _____

Signature: _____   Expiration *date:* _____ / _____
(required for credit card orders)

Colorado residents: Please add 3% sales tax.
Shipping: Include $3.95 for the first book and 75¢ for each additional book ordered.

❑ *Please send me a copy of your complete catalog of books and plays.*